WALTER WINK

WHEN *The* POWERS FALL

Reconciliation in the Healing *of* Nations

FORTRESS PRESS   MINNEAPOLIS

WHEN THE POWERS FALL
Reconciliation and the Healing of Nations

Originally published in Sweden under the title *Healing a Nation's Wounds: Reconciliation on the Road to Democracy* (copyright © 1997 Life and Peace Institute).

Cover design and illustration: Brad Norr Design
Text design: David Lott
Author photo: UMCom

Wink, Walter.
    [Healing a nation's wounds]
    When the powers fall : reconciliation in the healing of nations / Walter Wink.
        p.   cm.
    Originally published: Healing a nation's wounds. Sweden : Life and Peace Institute, 1997. With a new foreword.
    Includes bibliographical references (p.   ).
    ISBN 0-8006-3127-7 (alk. paper)
    1. Reconciliation—Religious aspects—Christianity. 2. Violence—Biblical teaching. 3. Church and state. 4. Powers (Christian theology)—Biblical teaching. I. Title.
    BT736.W55   1998
    261.7—dc21   97-46413
                                              CIP

The paper used in this publication meets the minimum requirements of American National Standard for Information Sciences—Permanence of Paper for Printed Library Materials, ANSI Z329.48-1984.

Manufactured in the U.S.A.   AF 1-3127

02   01   00   99   98   2   3   4   5   6   7   8   9   10

Contents

Preface

Suddenly, everyone seems to be apologizing. President Clinton recently apologized to the elderly victims of the infamous Tuskegee syphilis experiments, and to Hawaiians for the overthrow of the monarchy of Queen Liliuokalai a century ago. He is now considering an apology for slavery. President Bush issued a formal apology to the Japanese Americans who were interned during World War II. The Prime Minister of England, Tony Blair, went part of the way toward an apology to the Irish for the way the English handled the potato famine. The government of Australia apologized for the way it has treated aborigines.

Churches are also getting into the act. Italian bishops of the Roman Catholic Church have asked the Protestant Waldensians for forgiveness for the "suffering and injury" inflicted on them by the Catholic majority throughout the centuries. The Southern Baptists have apologized to blacks for slavery, and the United Church of Christ has done the same with regard to Native Americans.

Everyone, it seems, is jumping on the apology bandwagon. Words like "forgiveness" and "reconciliation" are no longer the preserve of the churches, but are entering the secular vocabulary, especially in those countries making the hard transition from dictatorship to democracy. In places like Bosnia and El Salvador, Chile and South Africa, East Germany and Argentina, people are struggling to come to terms with their former torturers and enemies. Should they be pardoned? Forgiven? Should they apologize? Be prosecuted? These questions must be answered in different ways in different nations. How much truth a society will tolerate depends largely on the new balance of power. A fragile and still questionable democracy may be unable to prosecute or even name names if the army of the oppressive regime is largely intact, as in El Salvador or Chile; whereas the numerically overwhelming black majority and the credibility of its new rulers made it possible for South Africa to authorize a Truth and Reconciliation Commission to accept confessions of human rights violations under the apartheid regimes and to consider amnesty.

Before a nation can get on with the routine tasks of nation building, it has to come to terms with its past. The church has much to contribute to the process of reconciliation. It can provide theological insights about the difference between true and false forgiveness, true and false reconciliation, and true and false apologies. When President Clinton apologized to the victims of the government's syphilis experiments, he was speaking to the actual victims on behalf of the perpetrating government (which had earlier paid the survivors and relatives $10 million, but without an apology). But when he issued an apology to Hawaiians, no reparations were included and no political restitution was envisioned. The first was a true, the second a false, apology. The first was made with at least a modicum of pain to actual victims; the second was a political gesture made at no cost that vindicated Hawaiian national feelings but did nothing to alter the actual situation.

It is timely, then, to spur a national, indeed, international debate on the role of truth commissions, forgiveness, reconciliation, restitution, and apology. This task is all the more urgent in the churches, since in some cases they (or some of them) were complicit with the torturers and oppressors. Repentance needs to begin, in these cases, within the churches themselves. Other churches were aligned with the oppressed, and now find themselves faced with the quite different task of reconciling former opponents into a society capable of civility and nonviolence.

This book was written for the Life and Peace Institute of Sweden as the introductory volume of a series entitled *Reconciliation and the Church in the Transition to Democracy*. It will be followed by a series of nation-specific case studies from Eastern Europe, Asia, Africa, and Central America. The overall intent of the series is to support the churches in their attempt to be faithful and effective agents of true reconciliation in confusing and rapidly changing circumstances.

Against Domination

The Reign of God

*M*uch has been written about the process of liberating nations from oppression. Less has been said about what a nation does when revolution succeeds. How does a once-totalitarian state move to full democracy? How do former enemies learn to work together? And what, more specifically, is the role of the churches in fostering reconciliation and national healing?

These questions are hard enough to answer in a particular context. They are far more difficult to address in general. The full answer about reconciliation, then, lies in the case studies that explore in concrete terms how reconciliation is being helped or hindered by churches in various countries that have recently overthrown political oppression or ended civil wars. It will be the task of this volume not so much to answer these questions as to indicate some of their implications.

Theology transcends every particular context, of course. Christianity holds out hope, not just for the local situation, but for the whole of humanity. Jesus summed up that universal hope in the expression, "the kingdom of God," better translated "the reign of God," since the emphasis is not on a domain so much as God's active sovereignty in the affairs of the world. The effort to heal a society racked by ethnic hatreds or exhausted by oppression can be helpfully undergirded by Jesus' message of God's reign. Otherwise we may despair over our failures to achieve genuine democracy, or (unlikely event!) become inflated by our successes and equate the new social order with the will of God.

No nation ever struggled harder to understand the implications of God's rule in society than Israel. Its long agony with kingship, its yearning for a righteous nation, its visions of a coming benevolent divine rule, were met by Jesus' proclamation that God's reign was indeed dawning in his own ministry. He declared the reign of God to be at hand, or even to be breaking into history already through his own words and deeds (Mark 1:14-15; Matt. 12:28; Luke 11:20; 10:18; 17:20-21). But if God's benevolent rule has already been inaugurated, *where* is it, *when* will it be consummated, and *what* is it like?

Where is God's reign? Already in our midst, wherever anyone is liberated or healed or exorcised or forgiven or transformed. Where is God's reign? In those struggles that attempt to recover freedom and human dignity, end violence and exploitation, and provide enough for all. Where is God's reign? Already inside us, in our souls, our depths, the moment we receive into ourselves the reality that Jesus proclaimed.

Thus the hotly disputed reading of Luke 17:21, "the reign of God is *entos* you" (which can be translated either as "the reign of God is *within* you" or "the reign of God is *among* you" or "*in the midst* of you"), is wrongly regarded as an either/or. It can only be both/and. That, at least, is how the earliest commentary on the verse puts it: "the kingdom of God is inside of you, and it is outside of you" (Gospel of Thomas 3). The reign of God cannot just be inner or outer; it must be both or it is neither.

When is God's reign? It is past, present, and future. God has reigned, reigns, and will reign. In the formula of the Book of Revelation, God is the one who is and who was and who is to come (Rev. 1:4). God's rule was manifested in the life of Israel and the ministry of Jesus. It has been seen, fitfully, inside and outside churches. It happens today, whenever people in the thrall of addiction or the power of delusion or the gall of hatred are liberated to their true lives. And it will come in all its fullness and power at the consummation of history. In an even simpler formula, God's reign is already present and at the same time still to come ("already/not yet," as scholars often characterize it).

When we ask, *what* is this "reign," however, the answers become rather thin. Re-reading the theology of the post-World War II era, I am struck by how privatized and blinkered was the German theology that dominated that period. Here was a generation that had been through the worst carnage in the history of the world, and they could write page after page with never so much as an allusion to the searing bloodbath through which they all had come.

I find this astonishing. It is clear that the "reign of God" of these German theologians had very little to do with the real lives of people suffering oppression, deprivation, or death. Instead, they spoke interminably about justification by grace, as if by constant reiteration they could persuade themselves that their complicity in or compliance with Nazism could be forgiven. Of course it could! But why not just come right out and *confess* it, rather than forever going on about justification by grace, as if the theological principle could work atonement without public acknowledgment of need? This judgment

> God is not simply attempting to rescue individuals from their sufferings at the hands of an unjust system, but to transform the system so as to make and keep human life more human.

may seem unkind, but it is relevant to the whole question of forgiveness and reconciliation that this volume seeks to address.

This highly individualistic post-war notion of God's reign was at last mercifully shattered by black, liberation, and feminist theologies. Born in situations of extremity and injustice, these new approaches have enabled us to grasp the political dimension of God's reign. God is not simply attempting to rescue individuals from their sufferings at the hands of an unjust system, but to transform the system so as to make and keep human life more human. The gospel commands us to pray for God's reign to come "on earth as it is in heaven" (Matt. 6:10). Our quests for earthly utopias, however, seem to end catastrophically, time after time. Very few people believe that the corporations, institutions, and political systems (the "principalities and powers") that grow rich at the expense of the masses will voluntarily relinquish their advantage. So many of those who have hurled themselves against the ramparts of evil have seemingly died in vain. In those rare cases where they have succeeded, moreover, the victors have too often yielded to the seductions of power, and the last state may be worse than the first.

Is the reign of God then just a vague hope, an idealistic picture of a desirable future that will never actually come to pass? Is it just a mythic cipher, a fill-in-the-blanks expectation with no reality to back it?

Perhaps it would help to excavate the origins of this "kingdom" language. "Kingdom" in the Hebrew Scriptures points to the most mundane of realities. It refers to the regnant political order: an authoritarian system in which the king ruled supreme. The Hebrew root behind king and kingdom means "to possess, to own exclusively." Kingship seems to have arisen for the first time in human history with the great conquest states, around 3000 B.C.E. As these massive empires spread from Mesopotamia, they brought with them what we might call the Domination System: a social system characterized by hierarchical power relations, economic inequality, oppressive politics, patriarchy, ranking, aristocracy, taxation, standing armies, and war. Violence became the preferred means for adjudicating disputes and getting and holding power.

Kingship was not, then, a primordial arrangement, but a rather late arrival. And it was especially late arriving in Israel. Having had their fill of the oppression of kingship when they were slaves in Egypt, the Hebrews attempted to develop egalitarian politics and economics. By means of the sabbath year and jubilee legislation, they sought to institutionalize their slave revolt. Under the sabbath year rules, debts were to be canceled every seven years in order to prevent foreclosure of land, slaves were to be freed, and the land was to lie fallow. Every forty-nine (or fifty) years, rural property sold to satisfy debts was to be restored to its ancestral owners. Much of this legislation was ignored in various periods of Israel's life. But the intention was clear: to prevent a vast disparity between rich and poor from taking hold in Israel.

Israel tried to avoid kingship. Yahweh alone would be their leader. Interestingly, Yahweh was never called "king" prior to the rise of the monarchy in Israel.[1] Likewise, most pre-monarchical houses were of roughly the same modest size, whereas after the establishment of monarchy there were a few large homes and many hovels. When the people requested a king at last, Samuel warned them of the consequences: an aristocracy, military conscription, a standing army, a military-industrial complex to make weapons, taxation to support it all, the enslavement or forced enrollment of sons and daughters to serve the king, and the seizure of lands and goods under royal pretext (1 Samuel 8). The people persisted, however, and the rest of Israel's history, down to the Babylonian exile, is the sad tale of power politics played out with all the intrigue and injustice of the pagans. Israel, called to be different from the nations, had become a nation like all the rest. It had entered into the worldwide network of principalities and powers that comprise the Domination System.

Israel's prophets began to look to the future for the end of human kingship and the restoration of God's direct rule. Or they dreamed of a new line of David that would avoid all the evils that David's actual line had caused. Not surprisingly, the hope for a future king or anointed one is infrequent in the Hebrew Scriptures. Having been burned repeatedly, many were ambivalent or downright negative about bringing back an institution that had been the source of so much misery.

The immediate context of the New Testament was not the Jewish kingship, which was defunct during most of that period, but rather the Roman imperium. The expression "kingdom of God" is actually fairly rare in the Hebrew Bible and the later Jewish writings. With the Jesus movement, however, that phrase suddenly became central. Against the kingdom of Rome the early Christians proclaimed the kingdom of God. Against Caesar's imperial rule they placed God's imperial rule. "Kingdom of God" thus needs to be seen in its political context. It is a counter-assertion, against the hegemony of the Roman empire, that Rome and its pretenders are not ultimate, that God's rule will prevail in the affairs of the world, and that Jesus' followers owe allegiance to none other than God. Like many other counter-assertions, however, "kingdom of God" was in time twisted into a legitimation of divine kingship, both of God's totalitarian rule and the totalitarian rule of God's regents on earth.

There is, however, an even more decisive context for the gospel. Rome, after all, was only the latest in a long line of empires that had straddled the world. It was not Rome alone, but the worldwide system of domination itself that was the problem. Jesus' message has traditionally been treated as a timeless, eternal, contextless teaching proclaimed in a sociopolitical vacuum. But his teaching and deeds are directed at a specific context: the Domination System. Jesus' message is a context-specific remedy for the evils of domination.

"Kingdom of God" always seemed to me to be an empty expression. It denoted God's rule, but gave no indication as to what that rule entailed. It was Riane Eisler, a Jew whose family barely escaped Austria after the Nazi takeover, who enabled me to see the world-historic significance of Jesus' proclamation of the God's rulership. Since the rise of the conquest states five thousand years ago, she observes in *The Chalice and the Blade*,[2] no one has articulated such a consistent critique of domination as the Jew, Jesus. The Hebrew prophets had, to be sure, already envisioned elements of his program, and Socrates had anticipated certain aspects of his critique, but no one came close to matching Jesus' perception of the nature of the Domination System and what was needed to replace it. That new alternative he called the "kingdom of God." In order to specify its actual content I paraphrase that expression as "God's domination-free order." Here are only a few items in Jesus' critique.[3]

Jesus against Domination

Jesus repeatedly condemned domination in all its forms:

> A dispute also arose among them [the disciples] as to which of them was to be regarded as the greatest. Jesus said to them, "The kings of the Gentiles lord it over them; and those in authority

over them are called benefactors. But not so with you; rather the greatest among you must become like the youngest, and the leader like one who serves. For which is greater, the one who is at the table or the one who serves? Is it not the one at the table? But I am among you as one who serves." (Luke 22:24-27)

Jesus does not condemn ambition or aspiration; he merely changes the values to which they are attached: "Whoever wants to be first must be last of all and servant of all." He does not reject power, but only its use to dominate others. He does not reject greatness, but finds it in identification and solidarity with the needy at the bottom of society (Matt. 5:3-12//Luke 6:20-23). He does not renounce heroism, but expresses it by repudiating the powers of death and confronting the entrenched might of the authorities, unarmed.

His rejection of domination hierarchies could scarcely be more complete than when he taught, astonishingly, "Happy are those servants whom the master finds awake when he comes. Truly I tell you: he will hitch up his robe, seat them at table [literally, 'have them recline,' as at a formal banquet or feast], and come and wait on them" himself (Luke 12:37)! What master ever behaved thus?

These are the words and deeds, not of a minor reformer, but of an egalitarian prophet who repudiates the very premises on which domination is based: the right of some to lord it over others by means of power, wealth, shaming, or titles. In his beatitudes, his healings, his table fellowship with outcasts and sinners, Jesus declares God's special concern for the oppressed. His followers are not to take titles: "But you are not to be called rabbi, for you have one teacher, and you are all students. And call no one your father on earth, for you have one Father—the one in heaven. Nor are you to be called instructors, for you have one instructor" (Matt. 23:8-10). His followers are to maintain domination-free relationships in a discipleship of equals that includes women. The hierarchical relationship of master and slave, teacher and student, is not to persist. "I do not call you servants any longer, because the servant does not know what the master is doing; but I have called you friends" (John 15:15).

Jesus' actions embody his words. According to the Fourth Gospel, Jesus washes the disciples' feet, a task considered so degrading that a master could not order a Jewish slave to perform it (John 13:1-20).

Economic Equality

Economic inequities are the basis of domination. Domination hierarchies, ranking, and classism are all built on power provided by accumulated wealth. Thus Jesus' gospel is founded on economic justice.

Breaking with domination means ending the economic exploitation of the many by the few. Since the powerful are not likely to abdicate their wealth, the poor must find ways to transcend the Domination Epoch while still in it. As a consequence, Jesus embraces the sabbath-year legislation and challenges creditors not only to forego interest, but to ask no repayment whatever. To those who wish to follow him, he counsels selling everything, and warns the rich that they have no access whatever to the new society coming (Mark 10:17-27). To the religionist's dream of being able to be "spiritual" and still amass wealth within an unjust system, Jesus pronounces an unconditional *no*: "You cannot serve God and wealth" (Matt. 6:24//Luke 16:13).

His followers were to begin living now "as if" the new order had already come, seeking first God's reign and God's justice. Jesus and his disciples lived from a common purse. The early church "had all things in common, and they sold their possessions and goods and distributed them to all, as any had need" (Acts 2:44-45).

> It is the poor whom God elects and blesses, the meek and brokenhearted and despised who will inherit God's coming reign on earth.

It is the poor whom God elects and blesses, the meek and brokenhearted and despised who will inherit God's coming reign on earth. It is the merciful not the mighty, the peacemakers not the warriors, the persecuted not the aristocrats, who will enter into the joy of God (Matt. 5:3-12//Luke 6:20-26).

In parable after parable, Jesus speaks of the reign of God using images drawn from farming and women's work. It is not described as coming from on high down to earth; it rises quietly and imperceptibly out of the land. It is established, not by aristocrats and military might, but by an ineluctable process of growth from below, among the common people.

In sum, Jesus is not looking for a kingdom for himself or anyone else where power can be wielded in order to *impose* God's will on the world. He is inaugurating a domination-free society.

Nonviolence

An egalitarian society presupposes nonviolence, for violence is the way some are able to deprive others of what is justly theirs. Inequality can only be maintained by violence. The root of violence, moreover, is domination.

Jesus repudiates violence. Luke depicts the disciples requesting permission to call down fire from heaven on inhospitable Samaritans; Jesus rebukes them (Luke 9:51-56) When a disciple cuts off the ear of the high priest's slave in an attempt to save Jesus from arrest, Jesus is shown commanding, "No more of this!" (Luke 22:51)—an injunction the church took literally for the next three centuries. Matthew has Jesus say, "Put your sword back into its place; for all who take the sword will perish by the sword" (Matt. 26:52). Turning the other cheek to a "superior" who has

> The last supper and the crucifixion display Jesus' nonviolent breaking of the spiral of violence by absorbing its momentum with his own body.

backhanded an "inferior" is an act of defiance, not submission; stripping naked when a creditor demands one's outer garment brings down shame on the head of the creditor for causing the poor debtor's nakedness; carrying a soldier's pack a second mile would put him in violation of military law (Matt. 5:39-41). These acts do not *at all* mean acquiescing passively in evil, but are a studied and deliberate way of seizing the initiative and overthrowing evil by the force of its own momentum.[4]

The last supper and the crucifixion display Jesus' nonviolent breaking of the spiral of violence by absorbing its momentum with his own body. What Jesus distilled from the long experience of his people in violent and nonviolent resistance was a way of opposing evil without becoming evil in the process. He advocated means consistent with the desired end: a society of justice, peace and equality free of authoritarianism, oppression, and ranking. His method and his goal incarnated God's domination-free order.

This is but a sample of Jesus' critique of domination. Jesus also directed that critique against the *law*, which was intended to mitigate violence and injustice, but which had been subverted by the Domination System and made to serve the powerful, the wealthy, and the shrewd. He prophesied the end of the *temple*, with its reliance on sacral violence and its depiction of God as requiring blood in order to be appeased for human sin. He broke with the laws of *ritual purity* by means of which Israel kept itself separated from the Gentiles; as a consequence, the church opened its doors to Gentiles without requiring that they first become Jews. He criticized the *family* for its role in perpetuating the patriarchal system. And most remarkable of all, he related to *women* in defiance of the mores of his society, declaring them full members of the household of God and equal with men.[5]

This, then, is something of Jesus' answer to the Domination System. The gospel entails more than these elements, of course, but they are precisely the ones most neglected in the church's accommodation to the Powers. Only when we see the Domination System as the context to which the gospel was addressed do we begin to grasp something of the content of what Jesus meant by "the reign of God." Where is God's reign? Wherever domination is overcome, people freed, the soul fed, God's reality known. When is God's reign? Whenever people turn from the idols of power and wealth and fame to the governance of God in a society of equals. What is God's reign? It is the transformation of the Domination System into a nonviolent, humane, ecologically sustainable, livable environment fashioned to enable people to grow and grow well.

The meaning of God's "kingdom" is thus incredibly simple: it is the coming of God's domination-free order. That is a message so elementary that even a child can understand it. For children it means, among other things, no more beatings; for women, as a bare minimum, no more battering and rape; for men, as a gospel imperative, no more exploitation, violence, and war.

Thus, while the local context is significant, the most fundamental context to which the gospel is addressed is well-nigh universal: the Domination System that has oppressed the earth for the past five thousand years. The failure of churches to continue Jesus' struggle to overcome domination is one of the most damning apostasies in its history. With some thrilling exceptions, *the churches of the world have never yet decided that domination is wrong.*

Even in countries where the churches have been deeply identified with revolution, there has been a tendency to focus on only one aspect of domination, such as political freedom, and to ignore economic injustice, authoritarianism, the immorality of war, domestic violence, gender inequality, hierarchicalism, patriarchy, and the physical and sexual abuse of children. We have tried to take on evil piecemeal. While it is true that we cannot take on everything, we have not always located our struggles within Jesus' total project: the overcoming of the Domination System itself. Jesus' vision of a domination-free order enables us to see every struggle against injustice, illness, and greed as part of a single front, and gives us a perspective that links us to everyone engaged in similar struggles.

> **Jesus' vision of a domination-free order enables us to see every struggle against injustice, illness, and greed as part of a single front, and gives us a perspective that links us to everyone engaged in similar struggles.**

Jesus' proclamation of God's domination-free order provides a framework for dealing with the role of the churches in helping nations move from autocracy to democracy. Far more is at stake than merely an orderly transition to a more representative form of governance: such moments in history open up to heavenly potentials. They are transparent to the possibility of the impossible— what led observers to call the fall of the Berlin Wall and Soviet

Communism, or the South African elections of 1994, "miracles." At such moments whole communities are capable of acts of self-transcendence. Some are able to subordinate their narrow self-interests, for a time, to the society's greater good. In such times, it is the vision of God's domination-free order that prevents us from acquiescing to unworthy visions, or accepting political compromises as anything more than temporary pauses on the path to fuller justice. It is the presence of myriads of individuals and groups, each acting and praying in their own way for God's reign to come "on earth as it is in heaven," moreover, that is the necessary but not sufficient cause for such miracles.

CHAPTER TWO

Reconciliation

What Is Reconciliation?

*D*uring such transfers of power, the churches have a unique role to play in fostering genuine reconciliation between formerly warring parties. The fact that the churches have often failed at this task in no way mitigates the importance of the attempt. The reign of God in human affairs means first and foremost that God has taken the initiative to reconcile us, both to God and to each other. Past complicity with the Domination System needs to be acknowledged. Repentance needs to be tendered so that God's forgiveness, already freely given, can be accepted. Old enmities must be healed, for unresolved hatreds can lead to acts of revenge by those newly empowered, so that the old system of domination is continued in the new. A clean break with domination requires an act of social reconciliation, for which South Africa has so far provided a superb example. As the political philosopher Hannah Arendt reminds us, human societies could not exist without forgiveness and the public acts of contrition and confession that make reconciliation possible.[1]

Reconciliation is more than forgiveness, however. Forgiveness can be unilateral; reconciliation is always mutual. One can forgive those who are not even aware that one has something against them. One can forgive a dead parent, or someone who caused injury or abuse decades before, wholly without their participation. Reconciliation, on the other hand, is more difficult. It requires that I and the other person from whom I have been separated by enmity, mutually forgive each other and walk into a common future together. Forgiveness is thus a component of reconciliation, but only a first step. We may forgive our enemies in our hearts, but reconciliation requires that we pick up the phone or meet face to face and try to work things out.

Forgiveness is one of the most frequent of miracles. I use "miracle" advisedly, for forgiveness is among the most unexpected and impossible acts a human being can perform, and yet people do it every day. Take, for example, a woman who has been tortured and repeatedly raped, who says that she has forgiven her torturers. How is such a thing possible? Does she not want to burn them with acid, dismember them with an axe, submit them to the same sadistic rituals to which they subjected her? It runs against human nature to forgive all that she has suffered. She has every right to demand strict justice, to see these persecutors tried and convicted and made to pay for their crimes against her. And yet she brazenly forgives them. I can find no other word for it: a miracle.

Leah Rabin, the widow of assassinated Israeli Prime Minister Yitzhak Rabin, speaks of how she has been reconciled with Yasser Arafat.

> I have a very warm feeling for him. You know he came here after my husband's murder. He was here in this apartment, and we spent a very amazing hour or two hours together. He couldn't have been nicer. It really was amazing, you know, that this person until not too long ago we thought we shall never reconcile with. And now he comes in like a member of the family and is accepted like one. What I am saying is that it is so easy to forget—to get over—longtime misunderstandings.[2]

Forgiveness does not mean that we condone or accept the behavior of the perpetrator. The victim does not turn a blind eye to the crime, but rather frees herself from ongoing psychological torture, thus clearing a path by which she can seek justice that is motivated, not by revenge, but by the pursuit of universal change and transformation. Harboring enmity and seeking revenge only perpetuates the power of oppressors to lord it over their victims long after the deed was done. Thus, at the most fundamental level, forgiveness spells liberation for the victim. This, however, is not the whole story.

> Harboring enmity and seeking revenge only perpetuates the power of oppressors to lord it over their victims long after the deed was done.

In 1988 I led a workshop on nonviolence with a group of South African church leaders, half of them black. Every black person there had been tortured, and all had forgiven their torturers. One reason they might have done so is admittedly pragmatic. Hatred destroys the soul, and no matter how deserving of revenge the enemy may be, to continue to carry the desire for vengeance is simply to roast in your own fire. Forgiveness lifted a huge burden off their souls. It freed them from the crushing weight of a rage that could destroy them. For their own sakes they needed to forgive, so that their souls could soar free of the power of the past to consume them, beyond the power of the torturer to continue to dominate their minds.

That, however, is not the way any of them described the process they underwent. The summons to forgive came, as it were, from outside them, as a command of the gospel that they could not avoid. Much as they wanted to hold on to the desire for "sweet revenge," they felt constrained by their commitment to the gospel to forgive. They could not *not* forgive, because they saw forgiveness as their fundamental obligation to God. They forgave, not for their own sakes, but for the sake of the other. They had to forgive the torturers because *God had already done so*, and was calling them to do the same. As the Sermon on the Mount puts it, "Love your enemies and pray for those who persecute you"—not so that you can sleep better at night, or to avoid an ulcer, or to achieve peace of mind—

but "so that you may be children of your heavenly Parent" (Matt. 5:44-45, author's translation). The incentive is the imitation of God. If we want to be like God, then we must act the way God acts. God forgives us, so we must forgive others.

Why clutter the simple act of forgiveness with all this theological baggage? Is it not healthier just to take care of ourselves, despite the enemy? Why not forgive so that we can sleep better at night or avoid an ulcer? Why bring God into it?

Because the goal of forgiveness is always reconciliation. Moreover, reconciliation means, finally, reestablishing love between two or more estranged parties. Forgiveness for my own sake is selfish, narcissistic, and private. God calls us to forgive so that the walls of enmity can be torn down—between races, between sexes, between nations, between classes, between neighbors, between strangers, between family members and friends. Reflecting on his own experience of encountering on the street and forgiving the man who had tortured him, the Uruguayan priest Luis Pérez Aguirre comments, "Only the one who hopes that his or her act will open a new history of fraternal relations can truly forgive the one who has shown hatred."[3]

> **God calls us to forgive so that the walls of enmity can be torn down—between races, between sexes, between nations, between classes, between neighbors, between strangers, between family members and friends.**

We must pray for the power to forgive so that we can reach across the divide that separates us from our enemies. Nonetheless, we are not bridge builders so much as bridge crossers, notes South African theologian Klaus Nürnberger. "The Bridge is already there—our Lord, who in His own Body of flesh and blood has broken down the enmity which stood like a dividing wall between us. He is the bridge over which we cross to each other, again and again."[4]

In the final analysis, we forgive the enemy for the sake of the enemy's own soul. The Greek term which is translated "to forgive" in the New Testament is *aphiemi*, "to let go, loose, set free, acquit, dismiss, remit." Notice that the direction is all toward the other, not toward oneself. By forgiving we set the other free. How? By removing from her or his shoulders the burden of our enmity. We free the other to deal with God. It is now up to them to encounter the living God with their own sin and guilt. It is now no longer a matter that presses on us, but on the other and God.

Are there not, however, some crimes so heinous as to be beyond forgiveness? Albert Speer, the only Nazi at the Nuremberg trials to acknowledge his guilt, declared that the Nazi debacle was so horrendous that no apologies were possible. But he was wrong. He *should have* apologized; he simply could not expect Nazi victims to forgive him (though they were welcome to do so if they were able). Jews themselves have been divided on the issue of forgiving the instruments of the Holocaust. Auschwitz survivor and Nobel peace laureate Elie Wiesel declared such forgiveness impossible.[5] At the other extreme, Rabbi Leo Baeck, a survivor of Theresienstadt who worked to defend the Nazi officers and guards from revenge in the aftermath of the war, actually prayed that God would credit all the loving and heroic acts of the Holocaust victims—"their noble dignity, their silent efforts despite everything, the hope that does not surrender, and the brave smile that dries up tears, and all the sacrifice, all the warm love . . . all the harrowed, tortured hearts that still remained strong and ever-trusting in the face of death and in death"—as a ransom for the forgiveness of their executors' sins. Thus the victims would no longer be their victims, "but rather a help that releases them from their frenzy."[6] It is difficult to imagine greater magnanimity.

Of course there is no way to "forgive" the Nazis for what they did; or Stalin, for the murder of twenty million of his own people; or Pol Pot, for the slaughter of as much as a third of all Cambodians. Judgment for such horrendous crimes belongs to a tribunal much higher than any we might convene. Christians, however, are confronted in such cases not with the limits of our feelings (Is it possible for us to forgive?), but with the nature of the God revealed by Jesus. "For God makes the sun rise on the evil and on the good, and sends rain on the righteous and on the unrighteous. . . . Be all-inclusive in your love, as your heavenly Father is all-inclusive" (Matt. 5:45, 48, author's translation). In short, God is incapable of not forgiving, because it is God's very nature to forgive.

Christians and Jews alike generally shape their liturgies around the notion that the first act leading to reconciliation is repentance, followed by forgiveness and, if possible, acts of restitution. In worship this often is expressed by the Confession of Sins, followed by the Words of Assurance and Pardon. We expect evildoers to repent and seek forgiveness. Jesus, however, reversed all that. He declared to an incredulous world that could not finally accept it, that God already forgives us, whether we ask for it or not, whether we like it or not. We can repent, in fact, precisely *because* God has already forgiven us. The gospel declares to us, You are forgiven! Now you can repent! "The kingdom of God has come near; repent, and believe in the good news" (Mark 1:15). It is because God already loves us that we can dare to approach God. God accepts us as we are; the prodigal son's father runs to greet him and receives him back as son. God, moreover, makes no exceptions: whether we are able to forgive or not, God does,[7] and this applies even to Hitler, Stalin, and Pol Pot.

Paul makes the same point in 2 Corinthians. Those who are in Christ, he says, are a new creation, because God has taken the initiative, through Christ, to reconcile us. "In Christ God was reconciling the world to Godself, not counting their trespasses against them, and entrusting the message of reconciliation to us" (2 Cor. 5:19, author's translation). As Jan Milic Lochman notes, *katalassein* (to reconcile) here is used only of God, *katallagenai* (to be reconciled) only of humanity. God is not reconciled. We are.[8] All we contribute is our response, by becoming ambassadors of reconciliation. That means that we must *initiate* the reconciliatory process, not wait for the former oppressor to take the first step. Such acts of reconciliation cannot, however, be demanded of anyone; they can only be initiated by the parties involved, responding, consciously or unconsciously, to the promptings of the Holy Spirit.

True and False Forgiveness

Nevertheless, there are gross misunderstandings about forgiveness that block the path to reconciliation. One is the old adage, "Forgive and forget." How this perverse piece of advice ever gained currency is beyond understanding. No one can consciously "forget" anything. The very attempt to "forget" something places it in the center of conscious attention. We should never try to forget our life's most painful experiences anyway. Forgiveness is offered with full knowledge of the offense. We must never forget the ways we have hurt others, lest we pretend to be better than we are, and we must never forget the way others have hurt us, if for no other reason than to protect ourselves against its repetition.

A second misapprehension is that forgiveness is sentimental, that it overlooks crimes and indulges wrongdoers. There are some wonderful stories about people who have refused to bring charges against those who have criminally wronged them. There are instances, however, when such forgiveness is itself criminal, releasing on society a sociopath who will simply continue to victimize others.

Doris Donnelly provides an instructive case. A car driven by the father of three young boys was struck head-on by a pickup truck being driven on the wrong side of the road. The driver of the car suffered injuries so severe that he wound up spending over eighteen months in a hospital three hundred miles from home, and his vision in one eye was permanently impaired. The driver of the truck was uninjured.

Early in her husband's convalescence, the driver of the truck begged the wife of the victim not to press criminal charges against him. An unemployed Vietnam veteran, he had a wife and two little daughters of his own to care for and was close to being hired as a school bus driver. This would be his first permanent job in four years. Moved, the injured man and his wife decided to forego the legal suit.

Several days later, the wife of the truck driver came to the hospital and told the injured man and his wife that her husband went on drinking bouts several times a week. These bouts occasioned an acute depression, to which her husband responded by careening down back roads in his truck, set on frightening the wits out of passengers in other cars. His favorite sport was driving on the wrong side of the road, forcing any driver who happened to come along to veer off into the trees or embankments. Twice she had been with him on these potentially lethal rides, and was convinced he was in need of psychiatric care, which she felt he would never seek voluntarily. Poor as they were, her greatest fear was that he would, in fact, get the job as a school bus driver. She hoped this accident would force the issue into the open.

This new evidence caused the victim and his wife to a revised decision. While they remained forgiving, they explained to him, they could not in good conscience allow him to subject school children to mortal danger. They pressed charges, which meant that his license was suspended for six months and he had to undergo a compulsory rehabilitation program in order to get his license back. The couple promised to assist him in finding a counselor and to help him search for another job.[9]

Forgiveness exists in tension with judgment. Parents routinely try to make clear to their children that they forgive them even though they find it necessary to punish them. Can such personal forgiveness be applied to nations, however? To a nation seeking reconciliation, does the coming of God's domination-free order mean that a society moving toward reconciliation and an eventual general amnesty still needs to consider prosecuting those guilty of formulating the policy of human rights violations and those most zealous in their perpetration?

Granted that criminal guilt applies only to those individuals who actually commit human rights violations, torture, and murder; nevertheless, all the members of a state are *responsible* for what their nation does in their name. Thus the individual members of a nation are judged collectively by God on the basis of how they treated "the least of these" (Matt. 25:31-32). Karl Jaspers distinguishes between: (*a*) criminal guilt; (*b*) political guilt; (*c*) moral guilt; and (*d*) metaphysical guilt. All of the citizens of a nation share *political* guilt for its wrongful acts, but most do not bear *criminal* guilt and should not be brought to trial. Each individual must assess before God her or his degree of *moral* guilt for complicity, accommodation, or passivity. Furthermore, all human beings, in solidarity, share *metaphysical* guilt for every wrong and injustice in the world, but especially those which might have been prevented by our acts. Moral and metaphysical guilt are not the domain of the state, but are the jurisdiction of God alone.[10]

Martin Niemöller, one of the first church leaders arrested by the Nazis and thus arguably one of the least guilty of complicity in

Nazi crimes, nevertheless declared, after the fall of the Third Reich, "We are all guilty." According to Jasper's typology, Niemöller was referring to political, moral, and metaphysical guilt (*b–d*), not criminal guilt (*a*), though in the controversy that resulted, many apparently understood him to mean the latter.

The gospel affirms that God forgives all sins, however heinous. Reconciliation, however, hinges on whether the victims are able to forgive or not, and whether a society, for its own health, must bring charges against at least some who are criminally guilty.

Reconciliation as Process

Reconciliation is a process with discrete steps, but in practice these steps vary from case to case. The victim may eventually forgive, but this act may be preceded by depression, rage, and the desire for revenge, and it may take time to work through these powerful and legitimate feelings. Many victims suffer from post-traumatic stress syndrome, and a call to forgiveness may be premature if they have not worked through it. As Robert J. Schreiter writes,

> Victims of violence and suffering must tell their story over and over again in order to escape the narrative of the lie. As they recount their own narrative, little by little they begin to construct a new narrative of truth that can include the experiences of suffering and violence without allowing those experiences to overwhelm it. This includes, in the first stage, establishing a kind of geography of violence and suffering; that is, bounding it so as to tame its savage power. The more that the violence is so bounded, the less formidable it becomes. Without such boundedness, it roams at will in the life of the victim devouring, like the roaming lion in 1 Peter 5:8, whomever it will. The ministry of reconciliation at this stage is a ministry of listening.[11]

At the very least we expect the offending party to repent and confess. Following the model of Jesus, however, sometimes the former victim takes the initiative and offers forgiveness before it is sought (Luke 23:34; Acts 7:60; Matt. 18:21-22; Luke 17:3-4).

Many people think of reconciliation as something that comes about only after justice is done. Some liberationists bridle at all talk of reconciliation during the conflict. No doubt they have seen church leaders disguise a bogus neutrality behind calls for reconciliation. Nevertheless, nonviolent activists have repeatedly demonstrated the value of reaching across the divide while the struggle for justice is still going on. Both sides will have to live together after the end of the conflict. When Jesus says, "Love your enemies and pray for those who persecute you" (Matt. 5:44), he is helping the oppressed recover their humanity by affirming the humanity of their opponents. Praying for their well-being during the conflict will make normalization far more speedy. Those who insist on waiting till justice is done to be reconciled may never be reconciled, for justice is seldom completely done.

Often reconciliation is initiated by the victim. It can, however, also be requested by the perpetrator. There is a well-known story about the Dutch writer Corrie Ten Boom that has long haunted me. After she was released from the camp where her sister Betsie died during the Nazi Holocaust, she lectured and preached on the need to forgive enemies. One evening she was greeted after her lecture by a man she recognized as the SS guard at the shower room in the processing center at Ravensbruck. "How grateful I am for your message, Fraulein," he said. "To think that, as you say, He has washed my sins away!" [Already this has my hackles up. *He* declares himself forgiven without offering any act of repentance or apology!]

Her reaction is quite appropriate: a sudden flashback to the room full of mocking men, the heaps of clothing, Betsie's pain-blanched face. But then she was back in the present: "His hand was thrust out to shake mine. And I, who had preached so often to the people in Bloemendaal the need to forgive, kept my hand at my side." [Good for her, I say; let him squirm! But no:]

> Even as the angry, vengeful thoughts boiled through me, I saw the sin of them. Jesus Christ had died for this man; was I going to ask for more? Lord Jesus, I prayed, forgive me and help me to forgive him.

[She seems to be trying to *appear* Christian rather than owning her feelings and confronting this man with his sin. I want her to stay in the process longer. I want her to relive the shame she felt standing naked before this man. I want her to feel the pain of her sister's murder. Yet she had no doubt dwelt on these things for years. In any case, I cannot gainsay what happens next:]

> I tried to smile. I struggled to raise my hand. I could not. I felt nothing, not the slightest spark of warmth or charity. And so again I breathed a silent prayer. Jesus, I cannot forgive him. Give me your forgiveness. As I took his hand a most incredible thing happened. From my shoulder along my arm and through my hand a current seemed to pass from me to him, while into my heart sprang a love for this stranger that almost overwhelmed me. And so I discovered that it is not on our forgiveness any more than on our goodness that the world's healing hinges but on His. When He tells us to love our enemies, He gives, along with the command, the love itself.[12]

Apparently the vitality of her spiritual life enabled her to telescope the process into an instantaneous inner transformation, in which she prayed, not for his forgiveness (which she knew was already a divine fact), but for her own. God did the rest. Most of us will need more time I am not proud to say that on two occasions it took me four years of continual effort before I was able to forgive persons who had injured me. The miracle finally happened, however, because, as Corrie Ten Boom learned, when God tells us to forgive our enemies, God gives, along with the command, the power to do so.

We are enabled to forgive because we ourselves have been the enemies of God and yet know ourselves to be forgiven. We are enabled to forgive, finally, because we *cannot* forgive, and throw ourselves on God's mercy. Yes, forgiveness is impossible, and yes, God does the impossible. It is a matter of faith for me that the Holy Spirit can empower us to forgive anyone. It is

> We are enabled to forgive because we ourselves have been the enemies of God and yet know ourselves to be forgiven. We are enabled to forgive, finally, because we cannot forgive, and throw ourselves on God's mercy.

especially difficult, however, to forgive those who still have the power to harm us. Perhaps there are evils so intolerable that one cannot forgive; these may be the offenses Jesus was referring to when he said that such perpetrators would be better off if they had a millstone hung round their necks and were cast into the sea.[13]

As Sheila Cassidy puts it,

> I know what it is like to be powerless to forgive. That is why I would never say to someone, "You must forgive." I would not dare. Who am I to tell a woman whose father abused her or a mother whose daughter has been raped that she must forgive? I can only say: however much we have been wronged, however justified our hatred, if we cherish it, it will poison us. Hatred is a devil to be cast out, and we must pray for the power to forgive, for it is in forgiving our enemies that we are healed.[14]

However difficult forgiveness may be, it is still not reconciliation. The latter has been much abused in situations of oppression, and it must be carefully defined to prevent this misuse.

True and False Reconciliation

Consider two opponents, one a powerful state armed with the latest weapons and partisan to the whims of the ruling class, and the other a group of peasants, miners, unemployed day laborers. The second group, unable to endure their oppression any longer, resist the state, which responds with violence—the familiar pattern of structural violence, leading to revolt, leading to repressive violence. At this point, high church authorities step in to "negotiate," as if both sides had comparable claims to legitimacy. But what is there to negotiate? The powerful will give up nothing, and the poor have no leverage to take it for themselves. In such a situation, the church authorities are simply acting on behalf of the powerful. They are saying to the lion and the lamb, "Here, let me negotiate a truce," to which the lion replies, "Fine, after I finish my lunch."

Niall O'Brien tells how small landowners of twelve acres or so in the Philippines would often find that their land was taken from them or encroached upon by big landowners who had influence with the government officials who issue land titles. The small landowner would receive a letter requesting that he appear before the barrio captain and meet his antagonist; the barrio captain would help solve the problem and reconcile the two.

The problem was always presented not as a case of injustice but rather as a case of broken human relations or a breakdown in communications. The job to be done was to *mend the relationship*, not to undo the injustice. Invariably the "little" man was clapped on the back, cajoled, reassured, and led to shake hands with his oppressor, although no reversal of the injustice had taken place.

For generations peasants have been browbeaten and duped by this trick. Sometimes a priest or bishop would be asked to be present to give an added air of legitimacy to such spurious settlements.

O'Brien tells about Maximo, a poor peasant whose house was burned down by a neighbor. After a good deal of discussion, the man who burned the house agreed to pay 150 pesos (about fifteen U.S. dollars at the time). Maximo was summoned to the barrio captain's house. There, surrounded by all the barrio officials, he was intimidated. Eventually he signed a document in English (which he couldn't read) saying he was accepting fifty pesos willingly. Then they gave him only thirty pesos (three dollars). Finally, to celebrate the reconciliation of both parties, they all had some Tanduay rum—for which Maximo was made to pay with the thirty pesos.[15]

Such perversions of the idea of reconciliation understandably have made it the dirtiest word in the vocabulary of some revolutionaries. Nevertheless, reconciliation is central to the gospel. God's domination-free order requires that we transcend hatred in the very process of liberation, for the means *become* the

> Reconciliation after cessation of conflict is made infinitely easier if the conflict has been waged all along with an eye to ultimate reconciliation.

end. Reconciliation after cessation of conflict is made infinitely easier if the conflict has been waged all along with an eye to ultimate reconciliation. As Gandhi saw so clearly, "Each single step on the way to the realization of a worthy objective must be a worthy objective in itself. Means have a way of inserting and integrating themselves into ends and of determining their ultimate pattern."[16]

True reconciliation can be subverted by a government propaganda apparatus that equates reconciliation with compromise, the toleration of injustice, and obedience to the higher powers (distorting even Scripture—especially Romans 13:1-7—to that end). Reconciliation can be even more grossly perverted when religious leaders in a revolutionary situation call for "peace," meaning that the oppressed should not disturb the false tranquility of a society built on violence. Alternatively, spiritual authorities may proclaim a message of personal reconciliation with God and neighbor that assumes that all social problems would be solved if only more people could be converted; or the religious hierarchy may pretend to be impartial when what is needed is solidarity with the oppressed. This false reconciliation was articulated by a South African church officer, who maintained during apartheid that "The duty of the churches is to be agents of reconciliation. That means we must avoid taking sides and be neutral."[17]

When church leaders preach reconciliation without having unequivocally committed themselves to struggle on the side of the oppressed for justice, they are caught straddling a pseudoneutrality made of nothing but thin air. Neutrality in a situation of oppression merely supports the status quo. Reduction of conflict by means of a phony "peace" is not a valid goal. Nor is justice adequate, for when the struggle for liberation produces only ephemeral, inadequate, or transitory results, people often turn to violence. The worst thing about violence is that it sometimes works, thus reinforcing belief in the myth that violence saves. The goal is rather God's domination-free order, and that usually requires that we *accelerate* conflict as a necessary stage in forcing those in power to bring about genuine change.[18]

Another example of false reconciliation is provided by Aidsand Wright-Riggins, the American Baptist Church's executive director of national ministries, who severed ties with the Baptist Peace Fellowship because the latter had declared itself in favor of full rights for homosexuals. Wright-Riggins commented that many in the denomination "had hoped [the BPF] would play a role of reconciler among Christian people who have differing positions on issues related to homosexuality."[19]

In other words, he had hoped they would not express solidarity with the oppressed. As the Filipino poet J. Cabazares put it,

> Talk to us about reconciliation
> Only if you first experience
> the anger of our dying.

> Talk to us of reconciliation
> If your living is not the cause
> of our dying.

> Talk to us about reconciliation
> Only if your words are not products of your devious scheme
> to silence our struggle for freedom.

> Talk to us about reconciliation
> Only if your intention is not to entrench yourself
> more on your throne.

> Talk to us about reconciliation
> Only if you cease to appropriate all the symbols
> and meanings of our struggle.[20]

One of the great stories of true reconciliation took place in Europe after World War II, when the Moral Re-Armament Movement initiated high-level conversations in Switzerland between French and German leaders. The trust that gradually built up in the spiritual climate created by the hosts was instrumental in the healing of the war's wounds and the creation of mutual respect and even friendships.[21] That experience must be broadened and applied now to the former Yugoslavia. Let us hope that by the time this book is published, a major effort is under way to establish dialogue across the abysses of hatred in that war-razed land, and that cadres of peacemakers from around the world are playing a reconciling role even as they help rebuild its shattered cities.

The dangers of false reconciliation are diminished when the revolution succeeds. In South Africa, for example, the victorious nonwhite majority now recognizes the urgency of reassuring the white minority of their safety and importance to the future of the nation. In that context, the behavior of Nelson Mandela has set a standard of statesmanship worthy of emulation round the globe: inviting his jailer to be his personal guest at his inauguration as president of the republic; joining hands with former president (and later vice-president) F. W. De Klerk in a public show of solidarity; and repeatedly calling for reconciliation instead of revenge.

Even as apartheid ends, however, false reconciliation persists. A white professor of theology addressing a multiracial gathering of church leaders at Rustenburg, South Africa, in 1991 said, "I wish to ask forgiveness for my role in the creation of apartheid, a system which I now believe to be sinful." A white participant joined a small-group discussion after the speech and was surprised to hear the mostly black members of the group criticize a confession which he had thought to be a constructive step forward. His colleagues in the group viewed the confession as a bid for cheap grace. "They've taken everything from us," one member put it; "now they think that all they need to do is say they're sorry, and we'll say 'you're forgiven' and they can go their merry way, released of all further moral obligations." Another said, "I don't want nice apologies so white people can feel good. What I want is for whites to join us in the struggle to dismantle apartheid and create justice." Reconciliation is a process, and the theologian was aborting that process by leaping over the stages of anger and remorse and the need for acts of restitution.[22] Nonetheless, the issue is complex. An apology is certainly preferable to silence!

The National Initiative for Reconciliation in South Africa was much pilloried by liberals and radicals for its focus on individual reconciliation without adequate attention to structural change, and much of that criticism was justified. In the encounter-immersions they sponsored between whites and blacks, however, many individuals not only came to love their Christian sisters and brothers across racial lines, but also came to see firsthand the squalor and indecency of the lives blacks had been forced to live due to forcible removals.

An especially powerful mixed-race liturgy involved people one after another confessing how they had been complicit in the sin of apartheid, and asking the forgiveness of the group. This was followed by a rite of mutual footwashing. While such acts were far from adequate to bring down the system alone, they required about as much courage as the average churchgoer could muster, and went well beyond what most churches were willing to do. Some blacks may have felt this ritual was a bit of cheap grace, but many of the whites were radicalized by the experience and went on to challenge the apartheid system. We know that the apartheid government was agitated by the success of these ventures, and tried to stop them, for they were part of the atmospheric change which undermined the legitimacy of apartheid.

Stories of genuine reconciliation are flashes of the divine in the world's darkness. They are testimonies of the living presence of God in the lives of people who have refused to let their sufferings dehumanize them. In central Nicaragua, a group who called themselves "The Mothers of Matagalpa" organized to support grieving Sandinista women whose children and/or spouses had been killed by Contra fighters. For a decade they had seen, and treated, the Contras and their families as enemies. Cautious contacts led to discussions and the discovery that everyone on both sides was weary of war. All were in deep need of the same things—jobs, food, and housing. Both groups of mothers—Sandinista and Contra—resolved never again to support war as a way of settling differences. The mothers even agreed to replace the pejorative word "Contra" with "the Resistance."

> **Stories of genuine reconciliation are flashes of the divine in the world's darkness. They are testimonies of the living presence of God in the lives of people who have refused to let their suffering dehumanize them.**

To symbolize and manifest their commitment to peace, they decided to build a 150-house community where members of the Mothers of Matagalpa and disabled, demobilized Sandinista soldiers would live together with Mothers of the Resistance and disabled, demobilized soldiers of the Resistance. With some international aid, the project is nearing completion.[23]

An exceptional story of personal reconciliation comes from Lincoln, Nebraska. On a Sunday morning in June 1991, Cantor

Michael Weisser and his wife, Julie, were unpacking boxes in their new home when the phone rang. "You will be sorry you ever moved into 5810 Randolph St., Jew boy," the voice said, and hung up. Two days later, the Weissers found a packet flung onto their front porch. "The KKK is watching you, Scum," read the note.[24] Inside were pictures of Adolf Hitler, caricatures of Jews with hooked noses, blacks with gorilla heads, and graphic depictions of dead blacks and Jews. "The Holohoax was nothing compared to what's going to happen to you," read one note.

The Weissers called the police, who said it looked like the work of Larry Trapp, state leader, or "grand dragon," of the Ku Klux Klan. A Nazi sympathizer, he led a cadre of skinheads and klansmen responsible for terrorizing black, Asian, and Jewish families in Nebraska and nearby Iowa. "He's dangerous," the police warned. "We know he makes explosives." Although confined to a wheelchair because of late-stage diabetes, Trapp, 44, was suspected of the firebombings of several African Americans' homes around Lincoln and was responsible for what he called "Operation Gooks," the March 1991 burning of the Indochinese Refugee Assistance Center in Omaha. (He later admitted to these crimes.) In addition, Trapp was planning to blow up the Weissers' synagogue.

Trapp lived alone in a drab efficiency apartment. On one wall, he kept a giant Nazi flag and a double-life-sized picture of Hitler. Next to these hung his white Klan robe, with its red belt and hood. He kept assault rifles, pistols, and shotguns within instant reach for the moment when his enemies might come crashing through his door to kill him. In the rear was a secret bunker he had built for the coming "race wars."

When Trapp launched a white supremacist TV series on a local-access cable channel—featuring men and women saluting a burning swastika and firing automatic weapons—Michael Weisser was incensed. He called Trapp's answering machine. "Larry," he said, "do you know that the very first laws that Hitler's Nazis passed were against people like yourself who had no legs or who had physical deformities or physical handicaps? Do you realize you would have been among the first to die under Hitler? Why do you love the Nazis so much?" Then he hung up.

Weisser continued the calls to the machine. Then one day Trapp picked up. "What the f___ do you want?" he shouted. "I just want to talk to you," said Weisser. "You black?" Trapp demanded. "Jewish," Weisser replied. "Stop harassing me," said Trapp, who demanded to know why he was calling. Weisser remembered a suggestion of his wife's. "Well, I was thinking you might need a hand with something, and I wondered if I could help," Weisser ventured. "I know you're in a wheelchair and I thought maybe I could take you to the grocery store or something."

Trapp was too stunned to speak. There was silence on the line. Then he cleared his throat. "That's OK," he said. "That's nice of you, but I've got that covered. Thanks anyway. But don't call this number anymore." "I'll be in touch," Weisser replied. During a later call, Trapp admitted that he was "rethinking a few things." Then, however, he went back on the radio spewing the same old hatreds. Furious, Weisser picked up the phone. "It's clear you're not rethinking anything at all!" After calling Trapp a "liar" and "hypocrite," Weisser demanded an explanation.

In a surprisingly tremulous voice, Trapp said, "I'm sorry I did that. I've been talking like that all of my life. . . . I can't help it. . . . I'll apologize!" That evening the cantor led his congregation in prayers for the "grand dragon."

The next day the phone rang at the Weissers' home. "I want to get out," Trapp said, "but I don't know how." The Weissers offered to go over to Trapp's that night to "break bread." Trapp hesitated, then said, "Apartment No. 3." When the Weissers entered Trapp's apartment, he burst into tears and tugged off his two swastika rings. Soon all three were crying, then laughing, then hugging.

Trapp resigned from all his racist organizations and wrote apologies to the many people he had threatened or abused. Two months later he learned that he had less than a year to live. That night the Weissers invited him to move into their two-bedroom/three-children home. They converted their living room into his sickroom, and when his condition deteriorated, Julie quit her job as a nurse to care for him, sometimes all night. Six months later he converted to Judaism; three months after that he died.[25]

The American nonviolent activist Gene Knudsen Hoffman observes that in every conflict she has observed, all parties to the conflict had been wounded, and that the unhealed wound was at the heart of their violence.[26] It is no surprise, then, to learn that Larry Trapp had been brutalized by his father and was an alcoholic by the fourth grade.

> **The American nonviolent activist Gene Knudsen Hoffman observes that in every conflict she has observed, all parties to the conflict had been wounded, and that the unhealed wound was at the heart of their violence.**

Individual acts of forgiveness and reconciliation such as these are indispensable in the healing of a nation. In places such as Northern Ireland, Palestine, and former Yugoslavia, it may take generations of effort at personal reconciliation before the work is done. But there are also difficult collective issues of forgiveness and reconciliation that must be solved as well: Should torturers be granted amnesty? Exposed? Prosecuted? What is the role of apology, contrition, confession? Can we forgive when the perpetrators not only refuse to repent but continue to justify their actions as necessary for national defense?

There are legal quandaries as well: Under what statutes may human rights violators be prosecuted? Many of their brutal acts may not have been crimes when they were committed under the former regime; in fact, they may have been regarded as laudable. Acts such as Nicholae Ceausescu's kangaroo trial and execution in Romania made a mockery of the rule of law that so desperately needed to be reasserted in formerly communist countries.[27] In addition, there is the role of the churches: What changes do they need to make in a changing society to more fully embody God's domination-free order? What contributions might they make to the process of reconciliation and the implementation of true democracy?

CHAPTER THREE

Issues of Reconciliation

Truth and Impunity

One of the most delicate issues involving reconciliation is what one does with human rights violators after liberation is achieved. Should they be covered by a blanket amnesty, given immunity from prosecution, allowed to go on holding positions in the police or armed forces, and treated as if they were only acting in the line of duty? Does Christian faith require us to forgive such persons and wipe the slate clean? Is such a fresh start requisite for national reconciliation?

Different nations have settled these questions in a variety of ways, from a blanket amnesty with no attempt at exposure of the perpetrators, to full exposé and limited prosecutions. Sometimes the revolutionary forces are as eager for a blanket amnesty as the authoritarian regime, since both sides have committed gross violations of human rights.[1] No amnesty should, however, be given until all the facts are out and the victims have had their say. Amnesty should ideally be the last step in the process of reconciliation.

Nevertheless, the amount of truth that a country can handle is not a function of peoples' readiness, but of the degree of continuing power of the police, army, and political apparatus of the previous regime. Journalist Lawrence Weschler comments on the longing for both justice and truth felt by the victims of torture, in which the desire for truth is often the more urgent. People do not necessarily insist that the former torturers go to jail—there has been enough of jail—but they do want to see the truth established.

Fragile, tentative democracies time and again hurl themselves toward an abyss, struggling over this issue of truth. It is a mysteriously powerful, almost magical notion, because often everyone already knows the truth—everyone knows who the torturers were and what they did, the torturers know that everyone knows, and everyone knows that they know. Why, then, this need to risk everything to render that knowledge explicit?[2]

Weschler suggests that what is needed is more than knowledge of the truth; public acknowledgment that is officially sanctioned is required. Over and over the torturers had asserted, "Go ahead, scream, scream all you like, scream your lungs out—nobody can hear you, nobody would dare to hear you, nobody cares

> **What is needed is more than knowledge of the truth; public acknowledgment that is officially sanctioned is required.**

about you, *no one will ever know."* The torturer needs to be certain that no one will ever know; otherwise the entire premise of his own participation in the perverse encounter would quickly come into question. Weschler continues,

> That is the primordial moment which has desperately to be addressed—and as desperately by the torture-society as by the torture victim: Who was there? Who was screaming? Who were those people standing by the screamer's side, and what were they doing? Who, even now, will dare to hear? Who will care to know? Who will be held accountable? And, who will hold them to account?[3]

And, we must add, where was the church?

Truth-telling may be more a therapeutic need for some people than a matter of justice. Whole societies can, however, be victims of torture, Weschler comments. Everyone is affected, whether they are political or not. Indeed, many of those tortured were not political. Thus, everyone is intimidated. The whole society falls to whispering, or simply to silence. Soon, self-censorship means that even subversive *thoughts* are repressed, and the nation becomes one massive prison.

That is why the truth must be told, whatever the consequences. Exposure of the Lie that has held a people complicit and complacent is critical in liberating a society to pursue a more domination-free order. Authentic existence is possible if one has exposed the Lie, but it is not if one is unaware of living under its spell.

"Most of the direct victims of the covert violent attacks and assassinations carried out by forces of the old apartheid state say that they are ready to forgive," writes South Africa's Sheena Duncan, "but that they must know who it is they are forgiving for what."[4]

The following are examples of how some nations have dealt with the issue of truth-telling. They are arranged across a spectrum that runs the gamut from no attempt at truth-telling whatsoever to full disclosure, limited prosecution, and the granting of reparations.

Namibia

Wolfram Kistner, speaking in 1992, warned Namibians against reconciliation without justice. "No reconciliation, no forgiveness, and no negotiation are possible without repentance. The biblical teaching on reconciliation and forgiveness makes it quite clear that nobody can be forgiven and reconciled with God unless she or he repents. . . . Nor are we expected to forgive the unrepentant sinner."[5]

In the light of our earlier discussion, we might rather say that nobody can enjoy the fact of their forgiveness by God unless they repent. Otherwise, repentance is a work that we must do to earn God's love. The issue, however, remains the same: How can we be reconciled to God if we do not accept the fact that God has initiated reconciliation and offers it to us freely? Likewise, we are to forgive *even the unrepentant sinner,* but the sinner is unable to enjoy the fruits of that forgiveness unless she or he acknowledges the need for forgiveness, and that requires confession and repentance.

> **We are to forgive even the repentant sinner, but the sinner is unable to enjoy the fruits of that forgiveness unless she or he acknowledges the need for forgiveness, and that requires confession and repentance.**

Namibian politicians talked a great deal about reconciliation after they achieved independence, but some observers questioned whether this was simply a way of papering over the crimes of the past. Gwen Listner, editor of the Windhoek *Namibian,* complained,

> Reconciliation was implemented without any stocktaking exercise, namely, an attempt to come to terms with the past. In this sense, Namibia would have been better off if we had had some kind of truth commission, where all the ugliness of our past could have been revealed by perpetrators on whatever side of the political fence. Namibians needed a process of catharsis and this was denied them through the policy of reconciliation. We are all aware the new government did not want political instability after independence, and saw reconciliation as the only way to avoid it.[6]

This places the issue in stark terms. Namibia presents a clear case of false reconciliation, a reconciliation bought at the cost of truth. The apartheid regime in South Africa had, however, reneged on earlier UN-brokered agreements on Namibia, and there was grave concern that it would continue to destabilize the country after independence. Kistner was right; reconciliation without justice—in this case, an accounting of the "disappeared," public disclosure of who was tortured, who tortured, and who gave the orders—was inadequate.

Haiti

Following the restoration of President Jean-Bertrand Aristide to power in 1994, teams of CIA agents roamed the country and recruited intelligence operatives, mainly from the ranks of the now-disbanded FRAPH, the dreaded right-wing terrorist organization established by the CIA. *The Nation* (8 Jan. 1996) reports that U.S. Special Forces also secured the release of FRAPH torturers who had been arrested by Haitian police. Early in the U.N. occupation (to which the U.S.A. contributed 95 percent of the troops), U.S. forces confiscated 160,000 pages of documents as well as videos from the FRAPH headquarters. The U.S. State Department initially explained that the seizure was "to provide information on groups believed to pose a threat to the Haitian government and people, as well as to our own personnel." The U.S. government has agreed that the documents belong to Haiti, but has refused to return them without first editing out the names of American citizens. The Haitian government has let the matter lie rather than jeopardize its chief financial supporter. A Christian Peacemaking Team, however, chose to turn on the glaring light of publicity by staging a solemn march from the U.S. Embassy to the Haitian Palace of Justice with delegation members carrying boxes marked "FRAPH Documents in Full." The march was overshadowed, however, by the news that the United States had released FRAPH cofounder Emmanuel Constant from a Maryland detention center, where he had been pending extradition to Haiti. State Department spokesperson Lee McClenny claimed that Constant's "return to Haiti would place an undue burden on Haiti's judicial and penal system." Delegation members pointed out that several other human rights abusers had been tried without incident recently, and that the United States had received from the Haitian government a guarantee of security and a fair trial for Constant.

The Christian Peacemaker Teams report concludes, "Under the guise of pardon and reconciliation, poor Haitians are being asked to forget the injustices done them during the 1991–94 Army-FRAPH Terror. As Christians, we believe that is wrong. Impunity for murderers, many of them apparently hired by the United States, is a foundation for future abuses in Haiti and is unworthy of the sheep's clothing of 'reconciliation.' True reconciliation means healed relationships in which the abusive behavior of the few will not occur again. This is our prayer for Haiti and the purpose of our work."[7]

Uruguay

Lawrence Weschler has thoroughly detailed Uruguay's painful struggle to restore democracy in the face of an unrepentant military. Well before restoring democracy, the military regime demanded and won a complete and unconditional immunity that foreclosed not only the possibility of legal prosecution but even of documentation of human rights violations. Although Brazilians were also unable to prosecute, they at least had the satisfaction of a total disclosure. Argentineans had only a partial disclosure, but were able to prosecute at least some of the top generals (though not those responsible for the disappearances). For Uruguayans, however, there was no relief. There was neither truth nor trials. Files that had been exposed in Brazil continued to be kept current in Uruguay in readiness for the next military coup, should one be "necessary."

There were a few bright spots. Father Luis Pérez Aguirre founded the Uruguayan chapter of the human rights organization, SER-PAJ. With only fifteen members, they provided a focal point of continuous resistance, despite arrests, and succeeded in publishing *Uruguay: Nunca Más*.[8] Though it had no official imprimatur and had no access to the military's own records, this exposé was an extraordinarily thorough survey of a large random sampling of former prisoners. Moreover, opponents of the amnesty law were able to mobilize a quarter of the nation to petition for a vote to repeal the law. Although they were defeated on the actual vote, the very act of resisting the regime was an enormous step toward the recovery of a democratic ethos.[9]

I mentioned above that the greatest horror of torture, according to Weschler's interviews, is the torturer's arrogant taunt: "Go ahead, scream all you like, no one will ever know." As Uruguayan psychoanalyst Marcelo Vignar put it, "This point about no one's ever knowing was the very subject matter of the torturer's discourse, do you understand? That's what the torture was *all about*. That's why an amnesty [without full disclosure or prosecutions] will be so terrible, because it will perpetuate the torture itself."[10] As Uruguay muddles its way toward a hopefully more democratic life, the screams will continue to reverberate, soundlessly, through the entire society, drowning out the sounds of apparent civility. A repressed truth of such magnitude will seep like poison into the moral water table, and will not dissipate for generations.

> As Uruguay muddles its way toward a hopefully more democratic life, the screams will continue to reverberate, soundlessly, through the entire society, drowning out the sounds of apparent civility.

Guatemala

Guatemala came a step closer to exposing the truth than Uruguay when, in June of 1994, the army and government stunned many observers by agreeing to the creation of a commission charged with the task of assigning responsibility for the deaths and disappearances of an estimated 150, 000 victims of the conflict. Some believe the army's abrupt about-face was due to the weakness of the Truth Commission. It will have no legal function, only six months to work, and will not be allowed to identify individuals responsible for war crimes. Human rights lawyer Féctor Méndez calls the Truth Commission "a mockery to the intelligence of the people and to the pain of the victims' families" and fears it will foster impunity, serving as the basis for a general amnesty.[11]

The Truth Commission will not begin its work, however, until a peace treaty is signed, which could be some time. The Catholic Church decided not to wait. Already, Jesuit anthropologist Ricardo Falla had carefully documented government-sponsored genocide in Northern Quiché during the period 1975–1982.[12]

In late 1994 the church decided to form its own "alternate truth commission," funded largely by the governments of Sweden and

Norway. Names will be named, not in order to submit the perpetrators to judicial processes but to encourage them to admit their sin and ask for pardon. Most disturbing to the military, perhaps, the study will not only present a historical record but develop an interpretation of the incidents and their causes and suggest measures to prevent their repetition. Those who are being trained to do the research are bracing themselves for government harassment and violence.[13] There is something fitting in the church publishing the names of torturers as a basis for forgiveness. Since the church has no authority to prosecute, and the military is not likely to allow any prosecutions anyway, the matter in Guatemala has effectively been circumscribed. It is unlikely, however, that the victims will be satisfied with this limitation. Like Uruguay, but with infinitely more casualties, Guatemala is a sea of blood with no outlet to the ocean.

> There is something fitting in the church publishing the names of torturers as a basis for forgiveness.

In mitigation of the violence, the organization Witness for Peace has accompanied returning refugees, and Peace Brigades International has sheltered human rights workers with their own bodies, providing an international presence that has effectively hindered the work of government-backed death squads.

El Salvador

A Truth Commission also emerged in 1991 as part of the peace accords in El Salvador. Staffed entirely by non-Salvadoreans under U.N. auspices, it named over forty individuals responsible for human rights crimes, including the Minister of Defense and the President of the Supreme Court, and recommended they all be removed from office and barred from public service for ten years. Rather than attempting a comprehensive report on all acts of violence, which would have been prohibitive, the commission focused on representative acts of violence. It fixed blame for the 1989 murder of six Jesuit priests, their housekeeper, and her daughter, and accused Robert D'Aubuisson, founder of the right-wing political party ARENA, of organizing death squads and planning the murder of Archbishop Oscar Romero and four U.S. nuns. When asked why the Commission of Truth gave out the names of the perpetrators of crimes, the head of the investigating team, Patricia Valdez, replied, "We found it unavoidable and essential, considering how the legal system doesn't work in El Salvador. The report was the only way in which they could be publicly put to shame."[14]

The Salvadorean military publicly denounced the report and the government refused to give it official status. Five days after the report was issued the legislature passed a general amnesty, but some of the recommendations of the commission are, nevertheless, in process of being implemented. Already, the democratically elected government, despite its ties to the oligarchy and military, has forced the retirement of all of the military figures named in the report. Small gains only, but no one expects El Salvador to bolt toward democracy at breakneck speed.[15]

Brazil

In Brazil, the military gave up power but remained in the wings, ready to step in if they saw their interests threatened. Unlike other military governments that were summarily removed, as in Argentina, the Brazilian military slowly permitted a relaxation that resulted in the establishment of democracy after ten years. Most of the disappearances and torture had taken place before that gradual opening, but the military was anxious lest its meticulously kept records should fall into the hands of civilian authorities after the transfer of power. Nevertheless, they never got the chance to destroy them. In what has to be one of the most audacious moves ever made against a military dictatorship, a Presbyterian minister, Jaime Wright, with the complete support of São Paulo's Cardinal Arns, managed the secret photocopying of the military's entire archive, documenting every detail of torture and every disappearance. The story has now been told in breathtaking detail by Lawrence Weschler in *A Miracle, a Universe: Settling Accounts with Torturers*. I am drawing from Weschler's account here, and from conversation with Wright in his home in 1982, prior to disclosure of the documents.

In anticipation of the transition to democracy in 1979, the Brazilian military proposed a blanket amnesty that would cover both those accused of political crimes and state security agents who were involved in human rights violations. Victims who had already served time and had been routinely tortured were to be lumped on a par with torturers and killers who had paid nothing for their crimes. This "clean start" would have meant, in reality, burying the past under a coat of sludge. Jaime Wright's brother had been "disappeared," however, and Wright was not about to accept silence. That 1979 amnesty law, however, provided lawyers with access to the archives, though only on a piecemeal basis, as they prepared amnesty petitions on behalf of their clients. Lawyers were allowed to take out individual files for a maximum of twenty-four hours. Wright and his lawyer colleagues hatched a plan to copy these records secretly. Cardinal Arns made it his personal concern, and offered to assume responsibility if anything went wrong. Philip Potter, the general secretary of the World Council of Churches (WCC), pledged clandestine financial support (which eventually reached $350,000).

Twelve lawyers began systematically checking out files from the archive on what they hoped would seem to be a random basis. Wright and his co-conspirators leased three photocopying machines and employed staff to operate them ten hours a day, seven days a week. This went on, undetected, for three years, when suddenly Wright realized that they had copied *the entire archive—* over a million pages! The secret was so complete that most of the people who had worked on the project did not know that they had been engaged in it, even when they later read the final report.

The copied files were regularly transferred from Brazília to Sao Paulo, where they were microfilmed. A courier was kept busy spiriting the microfilms out of the country, several dozen at a time, five hundred in all, as insurance in case the operation was discovered. Repeatedly, at the merest hint that their secrecy had been breached, the entire operation would be transferred to another hideout provided in some obscure church building by Cardinal Arns.

Meanwhile, the million photocopied pages were being boiled down to a seven-thousand-page report, which was then further condensed to a summary digest that was secretly printed. Then one day in the summer of 1985, the digest suddenly appeared on bookstands all over the nation under the title *Brazil: Nunca Mais (Brazil: Never Again)*. It created a sensation.

The military still possessed total veto power even as it was handing over control to civilians. In 1980 they canceled elections, and as late as April 1984, the army took over the streets of Brasília in a show of force. The military wanted everyone to know that there could be no nullification of the blanket amnesty and no prosecution of human rights violators. As a consequence, Brazilians had to be content with the full disclosure of truth that *Brazil: Nunca Mais* provided.

Normally, truth commissions do not have access to the dictatorship's records, and must take the testimony of hundreds of people. Making that testimony public runs the risk of falsely accusing persons who then have no recourse to a trial to clear their names. The brilliance of the Brazilian exposure was that no one was incriminated by the testimony of victims (who might have some axe to grind), but rather by the factual reports of the military's own recorders.

In Brazil, not only was prosecution of torturers impossible, but the new civil government itself never endorsed the *Nunca Mais* report. Yet knowing the truth was, in itself, a kind of victory over the powers of repression.

Moreover, for many people, knowing the truth is itself liberating. In the 1930s, when the famed Russian poet Anna Akhmatova was keeping vigil outside Leningrad's enormous stone prison day after day for seventeen months, desperate for some word of her son's fate, another bereaved mother recognized her and timidly approached her. In Akhmatova's own words:

> Now she started out of the torpor common to us all and asked me in a whisper (everyone whispered there):
> "Can you describe this?"
> "I can."
> Then something like a smile passed fleetingly over what had once been her face.[16]

Argentina

Truth alone is not enough, however. There needs to be justice as well. In Argentina, where the army fell from power in disgrace in 1983 following the Malvinas/Falkland Islands debacle, the civil government had an opening to do more than tell the truth. A few military officers were actually prosecuted, and at one point there were more than 450 military officers charged. A major tactical error, however, slowed the legal process to a crawl: the decision in 1984 to allow military courts to deal with their own and then, if the military courts failed to act responsibly, to involve the civil courts. Predictably, the military courts dawdled, equivocated, evaded, and finally sank into a mire of inactivity. Months, years passed. Meanwhile, the solidarity of civilians against the military gave way to factional politics in the style so celebrated in Argentina, while the military came together as a solid phalanx bitterly opposed to all prosecution. Four times, military officers staged attempted coups. As elsewhere, the military had in 1983 awarded themselves with a declaration of general amnesty (later nullified the same year by the civilian administration in Argentina); but unlike Brazil, they also successfully lobbied a further decree permitting the destruction of documentation related to military repression. The civil government was unable to purge the army or bring it under control. Democracy barely survived.

Meanwhile, the new civilian administration was faced with a bewildering legal problem: What were the lengths to which culpability should be pressed? They decided that those who tortured or killed while simply carrying out orders would not be prosecuted. Military law absolved subordinates for carrying out criminal orders, but federal law did not excuse them. The question, however, became moot because the entire military was guilty. Following the example of Nuremberg (where, despite its great fame, only twenty-four were tried, eleven executed, and another seven given ten years-to-life imprisonment[17]), the decision was reached to prosecute only those who ordained criminal acts, and those who carried them out in particularly abhorrent ways. Even that was too many. Jeopardy was reduced to colonels and higher. But this issue, too, became moot: the military courts simply brought the process to a halt.

Finally, in 1986, under intense military pressure, President Alfonsín secretly cut a deal with the military: no more prosecutions for officers in active service. In 1990, his successor, President Carlos Menem, pardoned even the few who had been convicted or were still being tried. In retrospect, had the Alfonsín government moved swiftly to prosecute a limited number of high officers and then declared an amnesty for the rest, it might have succeeded.[18] To many in the civilian government, it was urgent to establish an ethos of democratic institutions in which no citizen is beyond the reach of the law. An example had to be set to discourage future military interventions and to limit their brutality. As the then-Senior Presidential Advisor, Jaime Malamud-Goti, later assessed it, "Bringing army officers to trial is an effective step in the protection of individual rights. As a result, governments are morally bound to promote these trials, even at the expense of exposing democracy to the risk of a military rebellion." He continues, "In submitting to the criminal law, human rights violators, who earlier had been above the law, are turned into ordinary, accountable citizens."[19]

In 1983, the Alfonsín government established a National Commission on Disappearance of Persons. In just nine months the panel issued its summary report under the title *Nunca Más* (this later inspired the title of the Brazilian and Uruguayan reports). It listed 8,961 disappeared persons, hundreds of clandestine detention centers, and the names of over 1,300 military torturers. Because the commission had no access to (now destroyed) military records, its deliberations could not be complete. It could not account for the fate of most of the "disappeared" or establish who was responsible for the crimes.[20] President Alfonsín decided not to make these names public, on the grounds that persons should be incriminated only by means of formal charges brought against them. Given the fact that the military refused to allow formal charges (except in a handful of cases), there was a sort of informal justice when the report was leaked to the press and the names published.[21]

The work of a truth commission, of course, should ideally *precede* any considerations of clemency or pardon. Criminal prosecutions should also precede amnesties. Contrary to the behavior of self-amnestying military regimes, amnesty should come only at the end of a reconciliation process, when the truth has been told, representative agents held accountable, and a process of healing catharsis has been allowed to run its course. In country after country, however, the military has prevented that process of reconciliation from occurring.[22] Thus we are left with merely a rule of thumb: get all the truth and justice that you can as soon as you can. As the political scientist Samuel Huntington put it, "In new democratic regimes, justice comes quickly or it does not come at all."[23]

> **Amnesty should come only at the end of a reconciliation process, when the truth has been told, representative agents held accountable, and a process of healing catharsis has been allowed to run its course.**

In Argentina, sadly, the Roman Catholic hierarchy was solidly on the side of military repression. Catholic military chaplains actually blessed the murder of "subversives" as a necessity for preserving "Christian civilization." The preferred method of execution was drugging the victims and dropping them naked from thirteen thousand feet into the Atlantic Ocean.[24] Belatedly, in 1995, senior bishops of the Roman Catholic Church in Argentina issued a statement expressing remorse for not having done more to prevent violence and government human rights abuses during the late 1970s. This lame facsimile of repentance did nothing to heal the loss of relatives of the disappeared. Mothers of the Plaza de Mayo, an Argentine human rights group, responded, "The church knew that military chaplains participated at the jails in getting confessions from prisoners." The bishops did not "fail to do enough"; they actively supported a policy of state murder and human rights violations.[25]

Chile

The experience of Chile was similar in some ways to that of Argentina and Brazil. As in Brazil, the church in Chile took the lead in human rights defense. The Vicariate of Solidarity was the rallying point of resistance in Chile, and did what it could to document torture and disappearances from the very outset of the military takeover. Like Argentina, moreover, which actually initiated trials against a few military personnel, Chile has been able to prosecute and even convict some notorious perpetrators, despite the military's self amnesty. Among those convicted were secret police Director General Manuel Contreras and Brigadier Pedro Espinoza, who were implicated in the murder of Orlando Letelier in Washington, D.C., in 1976. Some thirty-four people, many of them public officials and active police personnel, have been sentenced for human rights violations committed during the era of dictatorship (1973–1990).[26] Some two hundred cases remain before the courts, and another eight hundred cases, although temporarily closed, could be reopened if new evidence came to light. Since virtually all such cases fall under the amnesty, there is little hope to win them; but the continuing legal struggle keeps the issue of military guilt periodically in the public eye.[27] As in Argentina and Brazil, however, the Chilean army retains the power to impose its will where threatened, so that the growth toward democracy and a civil society has been gradual at best.

In 1991, then-President Patricio Aylwin Azcar named a government commission to document human rights violations that led to death under the Pinochet dictatorship. Its findings were made public but a rash of assassinations led to the effective suppression of the report. The investigation attempted to establish the number of detainees who were "disappeared," and did not include those who were simply tortured. Nor did it name the perpetrators. The new civil government in Chile created a "Commission of Reparation and Reconciliation" to complement the work of the earlier commission by providing a modest but decent pension for families of the disappeared, as well as scholarships, health care, and military exemptions. Returned exiles and those expelled from employment were paid reparations.[28]

In none of the Southern Cone nations was justice fully served. But in each case, *people revealed as much truth and sought as much justice as they thought possible.* In fact, prosecutions are very rare after a truth commission report. In most cases there are no trials of any kind, even when the identity of violators and the extent of the atrocity are widely known.[29] As Weschler observes, however, the very fact that some torturers were exposed, that amnesty laws were nullified or almost nullified, that soldiers were challenged with accountability for obeying criminal orders, means that "torturers can never again feel so self-assured—nor their victims so utterly forlorn."[30] Churches have played or are playing a central role in the demand for truth-telling,

> Churches are playing a central role in the demand for truth-telling, and it is urgent that they continue this function in the future, because the very possibility of prosecution, or even simply exposure, may have a chilling effect on torturers-to-be.

and it is urgent that they continue this function in the future, because the very possibility of prosecution, or even simply exposure, may have a chilling effect on torturers-to-be. Indeed, in most of these nations, the churches and religiously inspired organizations like SERPAJ were the only institutions in society capable of acting independently within the military state.

South Africa

Unlike any of the examples above, South Africa has undergone a genuine exchange of power. Although the police and army have not been fully reconstituted, there appears little chance of a right-wing or military coup. Such an act would lead to outright civil war, and few South Africans relish the prospect. This means that the new multi-ethnic administration's Truth and Reconciliation Commission, established in 1995, has been able to operate on the basis of principle rather than fear. But it has had less than two years to handle a huge number of cases. The commission is divided into three committees, one to investigate, one to grant amnesty, and one to determine reparations. The commission has the power to grant amnesty to those who make full public disclosure of their crimes. If amnesty is granted, the slate is wiped clean. If not, the disclosures before the commission are not to be used in any subsequent court prosecution. If the perpetrators did not come forward by the cut-off date in May 1997, they will live the rest of their lives with the prospect of being hunted down or fingered by the evidence of a former colleague.[31]

South African Methodist Bishop Peter Storey tells of the pain experienced by the families of victims who have to watch their loved ones' killers detail their atrocities without a trace of compunction and then walk free. But Storey remarks that people are coming to see that even with amnesty, their tormentors are judged—that there is a difference between *impunity*, implying escape from accountability, and *amnesty*, which carries profound inward and social consequences.

> Some have decried the absence of repentance in many amnesty applications. Apart from the fact that this is a further damning judgment on the distorted morality of these perpetrators, the legislation doesn't require repentance, only the truth. If it did, it would devalue those moments when apparently genuine repentance has been volunteered. In one case, a police officer who masterminded the butchering of a number of families in an attack on a rural village stood and faced his victims: "I can never undo what I have done," he said. "I have no right to ask your forgiveness, but I ask that you will allow me to spend my life helping you to rebuild your village and put your lives together." It is in moments like these that anger at the unrepentant is superceded by a glimpse of something more: out of the horrors of the past, the TRC (Truth and Reconciliation Commission) makes space for grace, and the potential for newness in South Africa shines through.[32]

Since not every case could be heard and investigated, some groups of survivors formed *Khulumane* ("speak out") groups where they could share their stories, gain strength from one another, and decide what they collectively wanted to say to the commission. South Africa's Sheena Duncan states that all faiths are engaged in planning symbolic reparation and healing ceremonies, incorporating African traditional healing and cleansing ceremonies into religious liturgies on a mass scale. "My own hang-up about it all is that the grossest violations of human rights like forced removals, the

pass laws, Bantu education, and the homeland policies are exclud-
ed in the legislation from the definition of gross violations of
human rights. I know they could not encompass those but they are
the things for which there is no reparation and which it will require
generations to overcome."[33]

Other Responses

In cases where an oppressive regime has been thoroughly liquidat-
ed, and foreign armies are pledged to back up civil efforts to punish
perpetrators and collaborators, as in Europe at the end of World War
II, the very vacuum created by the existence of a countervailing
power from the past may invite revenge. For example, postwar Bel-
gium, France, and the Netherlands introduced retroactive legislation
that defined as criminal behavior what had not, in fact, been so
defined at the time it was carried out. These countries punished over
100,000 citizens with capital punishment, jailing, fines, confiscation
of personal goods, probation, lustration (removal from office), or
relocation. Rule of law was sacrificed in favor of a swift purge.

In the wake of the collapse of communism in Eastern Europe,
by contrast, far fewer have been criminally charged, removed from
office, or subjected to sanctions. In East Germany, tens of thousands have been fired from their jobs, 50,000 have been charged,
and 180 convicted.[34] Thousands of Czechs and Slovaks have been
named as "candidates for collaboration" on the basis of unreliable
State Security Agency files without a chance to defend themselves,
but to date only a few hundred have been forced out of office. By
1994, Bulgaria had removed from office some 9,000 top managers
of enterprises, 14,000 officers in the state security agency, 90 percent of government administrators, and one-third of all diplo-
mats.[35] Distinguishing between complicity and accommodation
can prove extremely difficult, and the communist purge trials of the
1950s have left many in Eastern Europe skeptical about the power
of the judiciary to provide justice.[36] Failure to pursue lustration,
however, means that the bureaucracies of some of these countries
continue to be dominated by communist functionaries who may
throw sand in the gears of fledgling democracy whenever possible.

The major difference between the South American states discussed above and the East European states is duration: after forty-five years of state socialism (which had some features that were admirable), many families in the countries of the communist bloc had at least one member involved in some compromising activity. To prosecute or fire a handful of scapegoats could in no way cleanse the past, and to prosecute or fire everyone who was guilty would render the state inoperable.[37]

Some situations are so complex that talk of reconciliation seems almost hopeless. It may take generations, even centuries, for the peoples of Palestine, Northern Ireland, or the former Yugoslavia to be reconciled. Joan Löfgren's study of Estonia in one of the volumes of the Life & Peace Institute's series lifts up another difficulty. In Latin America, she notes, transition from military to civilian rule did not involve restructuring the apparatuses of the state. In Estonia, however, virtually every aspect of state and society required overhaul. Communist totalitarianism meant the attempt by a foreign regime to penetrate every aspect of life, even private relations. The churches themselves are scarcely in a position to press for reconciliation, since they are embroiled in some of the sharpest disputes. Some ethnic Estonians aligned with Constantinople accuse the pro-Moscow orthodox Patriarchate of being an instrument of Russian domination. Pro-Moscow priests charge that the Estonian Interior Ministry's Department of Church Relations intends to deprive them of ownership of their church buildings. It seems impossible to settle on what constitutes "complicity" in a country where almost everybody had to report to the KGB for one reason or another. Does past membership in the Communist Youth Organization, which was virtually mandatory for admission to university, count as a crime, or simply an empty gesture? And how to deal with compensation when the state perpetrating the crimes no longer exists?

> Christians are commanded to love their enemies, not after justice has been secured (it rarely is, at least fully), but right in the midst of the struggle.

Löfgren concludes, "Justice is needed first before true reconciliation can occur." This is a sentiment with which people in many transitional nations would concur. Yet at the same time, Christians are commanded to love their enemies, not after justice has been secured (it rarely is, at least fully), but right in the midst of the struggle. Is it necessary to distinguish between societal reconciliation, which waits on justice, and personal forgiveness, which individuals are capable of achieving? Or is that simply a dodge to avoid taking love seriously? Are only certain saints capable of forgiveness and reconciliation, or is it a demand laid on all Christians? If Christians exempt themselves from the necessity of forgiveness, how can they ask it of anyone else? Unless reconciliation is built into the struggle from the outset, it becomes exceedingly difficult to appeal for it at the end. It is, of course, natural to hate and refuse to forgive. The gospel, however, is not natural.

Peter Storey commented to me on the difficulty of working in a legal framework with what is essentially a theological matter. Under the law, if you confess you go to jail; in Judaism and Christianity, if you confess you are declared forgiven. Pax Christi's Sister Mary Evelyn Jegen wondered aloud, in conversation with me about reconciliation, whether the church has any business encouraging *legal* redress for the crimes of human rights violators. If only a few perpetrators end up being convicted, are we not encouraging a form of scapegoating? And if thousands of them are convicted and executed, are we not encouraging a bloodbath?

In a situation such as that in Rwanda, where tens of thousands of people were directly responsible for hacking, burning, or shooting their neighbors to death, how can any of them be legally exonerated, and how can all of them be convicted? Already fifty thousand Hutus are in jails awaiting trial. In a case like this, where half-a-million Tutsi and moderate Hutu were brutally annihilated as a matter of deliberate policy by Hutu extremists, Jasper's distinctions between criminal, political, moral, and metaphysical guilt collapse. These people were guilty on all four counts. The new Tutsi-led government wants to establish guilt starting from the outset of the genocide; the Hutu defendants want to go back earlier to deal with Tutsi oppression. One wonders if the only way forward is full disclosure followed by a general amnesty; but the mood is for revenge, and that could mean thousands of executions. A new society cannot lay its foundations on the bodies of its enemies, however guilty.

I have provided only a sample of responses to the problem of truth telling in newly liberated societies. A study of the responses of some thirty-five countries that have emerged from repression has recently been published in three volumes by the United States Institute of Peace, to which the reader is referred for greater detail.[38] The limited sample above does suggest a number of rules of thumb, however:

1. The truth needs to be told.
2. It needs to be told completely.
3. If the threat posed by the old regime and its forces prevents full disclosure, then as much should be revealed as is possible.
4. The truth needs to be sanctioned by an official body. If the new government is too weak to do it, then it should be done by the churches.
5. At least the leading architects and executors of the policy of disappearances, murder, and torture should be prosecuted.
6. If they cannot be prosecuted, they should at least be publicly exposed.
7. Amnesty should not be offered until the truth has been told and, if possible, at least some of those most guilty prosecuted.

In sum, a society recovering from the trauma of state violence needs as much truth as possible. Truth is medicine. Without it, a society remains infected with past evils that will inevitably break out in the future. Domination cannot exist without the Big Lie that persuades the many to offer their lives for the protection of the privileges of

> A society recovering from the trauma of state violence needs as much truth as possible. Truth is medicine. Without it, a society remains infected with past evils that will inevitably break out in the future.

the few. Truthtelling not only exposes that lie, but establishes a sacred space where others may gather who will no longer tolerate the lie, as in the churches of East Germany. It is the responsibility of religious communities to see that the truth gets told and to provide that space. Those cases where they have done so are a light in our darkness.

The Place of Apology

The extension of forgiveness, repentance, and reconciliation to whole nations is one of the great innovations in statecraft in our time. It is as if these central affirmations of Scripture are being secularized and broadened to take in the collective life of entire peoples. José Zalaquett, a human rights activist who served on the Chilean Truth Commission, notes that the attempt to reveal the truth about atrocities, to prevent their recurrence, and to offer reparations, is "the same philosophy that underpins Judeo-Christian beliefs about atonement, penance, forgiveness, and reconciliation."[39]

One form of repentance that has recently gained impetus in international affairs is the apology. The apology of one person to another, or of the one to the many, has been extended to include the apology of the many to the one and the many to the many— even of one nation to another.[40]

It was mentioned earlier that the repentant Nazi, Albert Speer, believed that no apology was possible. In fact, an apology was essential. Even if it could not be accepted, humanity needed to hear a perpetrator confess the magnitude of his crimes. The one needed to confess to the many. It was up to the victims of Nazism to tender forgiveness, if they were able to do so.

Not all apologies can be accepted, however. The U.S. bombardier who dropped an atomic bomb on Nagasaki offered to attend the fortieth anniversary commemoration and make a public apology to the city. The offer was refused by city officers. The bomb killed an estimated seventy thousand people and devastated the city. "We understand his sentiments, but there are many atomic bomb victims who are still suffering and who do not wish to meet this man," said a city official.[41]

The response of Nagasaki's leaders was disappointing but understandable. The proffered apology was, however, appropriate. It put on public record the contrition of a person who had committed what he himself identified as a war crime, and that may be all that could be done. In this case, reconciliation was not, apparently, possible, but the very fact of repentance was a step toward healing, for it acknowledged that the official U.S. interpretation of the bombing ("it was necessary in order to save a million American lives") was no longer held by the person who actually released one of the atomic bombs.

Thus, an apology does not have to be accepted in order to be efficacious. It is possible for individuals who have been harmed to forgive the person who harmed them. It is another thing altogether, however, to forgive those who have harmed others. No one can forgive someone on another person's behalf. The dead of Nagasaki were not able to speak from the grave and forgive their incinerator. Thus, forgiveness that involves groups is much more problematic.

Nicholas Tavuchis tells of a formal apology made in 1986 by the United Church of Canada to the native people of Canada for past wrongs inflicted upon them by the church. "We ask you to forgive us," the church's moderator told a gathering of native elders representing Indian tribes across Canada. "In our zeal to tell you about Jesus Christ, we were blind to your spirituality. We imposed our civilization on you as a condition for accepting our gospel." The chair of the church's National Native Council responded by telling the gathering that "the happiness felt in the council tepee was almost unbelievable" when it was learned that the church would issue an apology.

Two years later, however, at the next General Council of the United Church, the governing council for native peoples officially responded to the apology by acknowledging it but not accepting it. The oppression Native Americans had received at the hands of the church could not be overcome by words alone. "These are difficult things to heal," said the speaker for the council.

Rather than being a damper or rejection, this "acknowledgment without acceptance" served as the basis for greater dignity and autonomy for Native Americans in the United Church. The genuine contrition of the white majority meant that both sides now recognized the need for healing, and that there would be no "healing lightly" (Jer. 6:14), but rather a long process of deliberate restitution and consciousness-raising. In this case, then, acknowledgment but nonacceptance provided the foundation for the process of reconciliation. The fact that the majority whites had initiated the apology in evident good faith served as a pledge that future relations would be guided by a desire for restitution rather than by majority rule. Tavuchis concludes that the principle function of an apology is precisely its putting in the public record a statement of awareness and intent that seeks reconciliation, whether it has the power to accomplish that or not, and whether it is accepted or not.[42]

> **The principle function of an apology is precisely its putting in the public record a statement of awareness and intent that seeks reconciliation, whether it has the power to accomplish that or not, and whether it is accepted or not.**

Moreover, the United Church of Christ in the U.S.A. issued a formal apology to the natives of Hawaii in 1993 on the one hundredth anniversary of the illegal overthrow of the Hawaiian nation. The natives objected that words were not enough; there needed to be redress. In 1996 the church agreed to pay over one million dollars as a beginning. Reconciliation services were held that year on all the islands in very Hawaiian fashion.

Accepting an apology and granting forgiveness are also not the same thing. An apology is a statement of regret that attempts to elicit an act of forgiveness. Nonetheless, because it is often made long after the crime by those who did not commit the crime, to those who were not themselves the direct victims, it may not be possible for the survivors or their descendants to accept it. As was said earlier, no one can grant forgiveness on another person's behalf. An apology is a strategic move which attempts to absolve the injuring party of further culpability. It may be that the apology must be left suspended until the right thing is done. Jesus' statement, "I have not come to bring peace, but a sword" (Matt. 10:34), may have application here. A degree of alienation may be necessary in order to motivate, not just contrition, but changed behavior. The premature acceptance of a tendered apology may, in fact, abort the steps of restitution necessary for full reconciliation.

Apologies by nations seem to be a fairly recent phenomenon, and may indicate a small step toward maturity by the human race. The German churches made repeated attempts, finally arriving at a full apology to the Jews and other victims of Nazism.[43] Václav Havel showed his stature by surprisingly apologizing for the expulsion of Germans from the Sudetenland by Czechs after World War II. (This apology, one of the first acts of his presidency in Czechoslovakia, created an uproar. His fellow Czechs did not display the same level of maturity.[44]) President Bill Clinton apologized to the victims of radiation experiments conducted on them decades earlier without their knowledge or consent.[45] The Catholic and Anglican Primates of Ireland stood side by side for the first time in England's Canterbury Cathedral in January 1995 and appealed to the people of Northern Ireland and Britain to forgive each other.[46] The President of Switzerland apologized in 1996 to Jews for not offering to shelter them from the Nazis in the cathedral of Bern, and the Polish government apologized fifty years after the fact for a pogrom carried out in 1946 in which forty Jews were killed.[47]

U.S. Vietnam veterans have tried to find meaningful ways to apologize to their Vietnamese victims, including acts of restitution such as returning to the area of combat and rebuilding structures they had helped destroy.[48] (Has anything like this ever been done before?)

Eric Lomax, a British soldier brutally tortured in Burma as a prisoner in World War II, discovered the whereabouts of the Japanese man who served as interpreter during his prolonged interrogation—a man whom he would have been happy to murder earlier, but whom he now sought out to forgive. They began correspondence, culminating in a meeting at the bridge on the River Kwai in 1993. His interrogator was genuinely awash with guilt, trembling and in tears when they first met. "He was saying over and over, 'I am very, very sorry,'" wrote Lomax in *The Railway Man*.[49] The Japanese man had assisted Allied forces after the war to discover mass burial sites along the notorious Burma railroad. He often battled crippling depression, and had occasionally contemplated suicide. When they parted, Lomax pressed into his hands a letter affirming his total forgiveness. "I haven't forgiven Japan as a nation," Lomax said, "but I've forgiven one man, because he's experienced such great personal regret."[50]

The issue of forgiving Japan has been much in the press of late. In 1995, Japanese Prime Minister Tomiichi Murayama, a pacifist, finding himself unable to push a resolution of apology through parliament, simply apologized to Asian countries subjected to Japanese aggression and colonial rule. Not surprisingly, his action was attacked by some in his own government. Not all of the victims were satisfied, either. Some Filipinos argued that financial compensation is still required.[51]

What the Japanese do not seem willing to apologize for, however, is the surprise attack on Pearl Harbor in 1941. Nor do American politicians seem disposed to apologize for the bombing of Hiroshima and Nagasaki, though Hawaii's Democratic Party convention in 1994 called on President Clinton to do just that. In the absence of official conciliation, the Yokohama Association of Bereaved Families of War published in 1991 an open letter in U.S. newspapers apologizing for Pearl Harbor, and ended by urging people on both sides to pardon each other, be reconciled, "deepen our unexpected friendship all the more," and work together for world peace.[52]

Reciprocally, in 1995 the U.S. Fellowship of Reconciliation collected eight thousand signatures on a statement of penance for using nuclear bombs, and sent a nine-person delegation to Hiroshima and Nagasaki. There they presented the signatures at a conference commemorating the fiftieth anniversary of the bombing. On the way to Japan they stopped at Pearl Harbor and held a service of remembrance there as well.

One of the most deplorable moments in U.S. history was the internment of 120,000 people of Japanese ancestry during World War II. It took until 1976 for the U.S. government to officially apologize, and twelve more years for Congress to authorize a fund of $1.2 billion for payments of $20,000 each to the sixty thousand or more internees still alive, and to establish a foundation of $50 million for the promotion of the cultural and historical concerns of Japanese Americans. It required a further two years to issue the checks. Not breathtaking justice, but still an appropriate and extraordinarily rare act: official public apology with restitution.[53]

New as these acts of national contrition are, they are integral to the Judeo-Christian tradition. Citing the example of Jonah, Jesus said, "The people of Nineveh will rise up at the judgment with this generation and condemn it, because they repented at the proclamation of Jonah, and see, something greater than Jonah is here" (Matt. 12:41). "Woe to you, Chorazin! Woe to you, Bethsaida! For if the deeds of power done in you had been done in Tyre and Sidon, they would have repented long ago in sackcloth and ashes . . ." (Matt. 11:21-22). The ancient prophetic idea of whole cities and nations repenting is one that is just now becoming operational, and it is one of the great achievements of our time.[54]

CHAPTER FOUR

Toward *Democracy*

*I*n South Africa, where many Christians, black and some white, have spent their entire lives fighting against apartheid, the move toward democracy has created a vocational crisis. After decades of adversarial relations with the government and police, they now find themselves in political office or schools or the housing ministry trying to change the system so that it really works for everyone. What new kinds of responses are needed to help institutions that *want* to change? This problem is now being faced around the world, and it demands a new ethos, new strategies, and new thinking.

In significant ways, democracy is nonviolence institutionalized. The moment of transition from authoritarian rule to democracy may not demand the more heroic forms of nonviolent direct action, such as civil disobedience, hunger strikes, boycotts, sanctions, funeral demonstrations, blockades, no-shows, slowdowns, and so forth. If we think of nonviolence as a continuum moving from the fairly innocuous (writing to one's representative, voting, signing petitions, and so forth) to the moderate (mediation, conciliation, third-party negotiation) to the most extreme (lying in the runway before a B-1 bomber, sitting on railroad tracks to prevent shipment of weapons to oppressive military regimes, fasting to death), the shift to democracy will probably require actions at the more innocuous end of the spectrum.

I recently spoke by telephone to a friend in South Africa. "Everyone is in meetings, all the time. We are being meetinged to death!" What a nice change. And those meetings have been facilitated by thousands of citizens who are determined to seize the opportunity, an opportunity which that country may never have again.

One "buffer" in South Africa has been the National Peace Accord, led by church and business leaders set on avoiding the collapse of the peace process into chaos and civil war. This entailed getting representatives of all the actors on the public scene together in groups all over the nation and staying at the table, month after month, until trust could begin to develop and agreements be made. This process is credited by some with helping contain the violence between the contending Inkatha and African National Congress (ANC) parties to just two areas, Natal and the Rand. The National Peace Accord participated in training thousands of peace monitors who played key roles in the elections and in averting a bloodbath in the demonstrations following the assassination of Chris Hani, head of the Communist Party and next only to Mandela in popularity among blacks. "The Accord held the country together for two years," Peter Storey told me. "It was for many the first time they had sat down and listened to people of other factions." He himself sat on the Johannesburg regional committee with the colonel whose job had earlier been to harass him.[1]

Another important role has been played by the intensive training of grass roots leaders such as the Empowering for Reconciliation with Justice (ERJ) Project in South Africa, which trained thirteen hundred people in the skills of mediation, negotiation, and proactive peacemaking. These training events have prepared participants to engage in conflict resolution in their own communities and to act as intervenors in conflicts elsewhere. Those trained will train others in order to develop a critical mass of people who will demand and implement a nonviolent culture of tolerance and negotiation.[2]

Though little known, these two groups saved lives, curtailed destruction of property, reduced violence, and over a three-year period helped contribute to a shift in climate that nurtured hope and reconstruction in much of the country. Other factors may have played a larger role, such as the reconciling approach of Nelson Mandela, the breakdown of "cold war" ideologies, the successful electoral process and installation of a representative Government of National Unity, and concerted efforts by the South African Council of Churches, the Catholic Bishops Conference, unions, and other organizations. Nevertheless, the National Peace Accords and ERJ have been like the springs on a car: they don't make it run, but they certainly ease the bumps sustained in a period of radical social change.

Now the task for the church in South Africa, I am told, is to maintain "critical solidarity," not succumbing to the temptation to be court priests but not lapsing into privatism either. Critical solidarity: that might well serve as a watchword for all churches ministering in the zone between oppression and democracy.[3] This might mean fostering relationships with government leaders while resisting the temptation to cozy up to power. It would require that the churches continually represent those on the margins who are without adequate power or representation. It will mean exposing official corruption without regard for consequences, denouncing the use of high office for personal enrich-

> In many countries, churches cling to traditional authoritarianism, and are a hindrance rather than a help to democratization.

ment, and condemning the inevitable acts of cronyism, pork-barreling, and favoritism that are attendant on all politics.

One task the churches can undertake as the nation moves toward democracy is to increase the democracy in church structures themselves, including the ordination of women, the development of more representative and participative styles of church governance, and the repudiation of patriarchy. In many countries, churches cling to traditional authoritarianism, and are a hindrance rather than a help to democratization. It would be a major gift to the world if the churches would at long last condemn domination in all its forms, so that they may more adequately preach and embody Jesus' vision of God's domination-free order.

Democracy, as we mentioned before, is not the equivalent of God's reign. As countries move toward more democratic forms, it is important to stress that democracy as we know it is far from adequate. I am not referring to the way the term "democracy" is applied to every kind of despotism to lend a patina of legitimacy (as in the "German Democratic Republic" in East Germany or the whites-only "herrenvolk democracy" in South Africa). I mean the failure to achieve genuine democracy in every facet of life, from the family to church to education to the workplace to government at all levels. "Representative" democracy has, in countries like the United States, become more and more unrepresentative. Business interests overwhelm parliaments, people do not bother to vote, corruption is rife, and oligarchies of the rich run the show from backstage.

Those who have exhausted themselves in liberation struggles may find the eternal vigilance required to build democracy an unexpected drain on energy. The end of political oppression does not bring in its train the end of economic oppression. In fact, it may only deepen economic disparities. What is needed is a *process* for the democratization of institutions of every kind.

> The end of political oppression does not bring in its train the end of economic oppression. In fact, it may only deepen economic disparities.

Curiously, one source of help is emerging from within the U.S. business community itself. For several decades now there has been movement toward "quality circles," where all the workers in a given section give feedback on improving productivity, and often rotate positions to avoid the mind-numbing repetition that dogs assembly-line workers. A more recent development are "Large-Group Interventions" or "Critical Mass Events," in which consultants try to involve all the stakeholders in a system, from workers, janitors, management, and sales personnel to labor leaders, customers, neighbors, and city officials in the redesign of operations. In large-group interventions, emphasis shifts from managerial excellence (managing better) to transformational leadership (creating a new vision),[4] and from domination hierarchies to enabling hierarchies.[5] The corporate culture has to change in order to allow managers to become more participative, and to persuade everyone else that their input is significant—and safe to make.[6] The goal is to bring the whole system into the room and learn from it.

These large-group interventions provide a model for ongoing corporate decision making. They have even been applied to whole cities (Santa Cruz, California; Danbury, Connecticut). The democratization of businesses, government agencies, and churches not only complies with democratic ideals, it is economically more sound, organizationally more effective, and humanly more benevolent. Remarkably, the values implicit in large-group interventions are similar to those cherished by some traditional societies, where the "chief" merely states the emerging consensus, and all stakeholders have a voice.[7]

After all these centuries, it is time to consider the implications of Jesus' teachings on nonviolence and egalitarianism for the workplace. What would it mean to overcome domination in a corporation? What is the role of intercessory prayer in changing the atmosphere or ethos of an office, a city, a nation? How can we challenge these Powers to conceive their vocations as

> **This is a time crying out for innovation and experimentation in making societies more democratic. How can we reduce the growing gulf between rich and poor, the decline of the middle class, the shortage of low-cost housing, the degradation of the environment?**

service to the general good? From a position of "critical solidarity," how might the churches attack the greed that perverts our economic life?[8]

This is a time crying out for innovation and experimentation in making societies more democratic. How can we reduce the growing gulf between rich and poor, the decline of the middle class, the shortage of low-cost housing, the degradation of the environment? What can we learn from models that have already been tried and proven successful—Sweden, Mondragon, land trusts, base communities, nongovernmental organizations, U.N. peacekeepers? Powerful interests are set against economic justice. How can they be neutralized? And especially, what can churches do to alter the social climate from cutthroat covetousness to compassion, care, and conviction?

These, then, are some of the questions and issues the churches face as they minister to nations in transition from autocracy to democracy. In that ministry, the churches are not the handmaidens of government, operating to provide ideological consent and to create an atmosphere of compliance. The churches bear the imperishable message of the gospel, the coming of God's domination-free order. No political system can ever fully institutionalize Jesus' values of equality, nonviolence, and the rejection of domination in all its forms. Some, however, have done considerably better than others. It is the church's ongoing prophetic and pastoral task to lift up Jesus' vision of the reign of God in human societies, and to bend our societies toward that vision to the limit of our ability.

Notes

Chapter One: Against Domination

1. G. Von Rad, *"Basileus," Theological Dictionary of the New Testament*, vol. 1, ed. Gerhard Kittel (Grand Rapids: Wm. B. Eerdmans, 1964), 570.

2. R. Eisler, *The Chalice and the Blade* (San Francisco: Harper & Row, 1987), 120–24. She has honed and clarified her thesis in *Sacred Pleasure* (San Francisco: HarperSanFrancisco, 1995).

3. In the analysis of Jesus' teaching that follows I have not attempted to maintain a careful distinction between statements and deeds that are authentic to Jesus and those ascribed to him by the church, so long as they both reflect the values of partnership and reject the system of domination. Using Jesus' critique of the Domination System as a perceptual lens enables us to recover emphases lost as the gospel was domesticated by the early church. Although occasionally Jesus' teachings were further radicalized (as in Stephen's attack on the Temple in Acts 7 or the extension of the mission to include Gentiles), the main tendency of the tradition

(as in the Pastoral Epistles) was to accommodate the gospel in significant ways to structures of domination. Using the critique of domination as a standard does not replace the historical criteria worked out with such care by New Testament scholars; it confirms and supplements them.

4. I have developed this theme at some length in my book *Engaging the Powers: Discernment and Resistance in a World of Domination* (Minneapolis: Fortress Press, 1992), chap. 9.

5. All this is treated in considerably more detail in my *Engaging the Powers*. See also my article, "The Kingdom: God's Domination-free Order," *Weavings* 10 (Jan./Feb. 1995): 6–15.

Chapter Two: Reconciliation

1. Hannah Arendt, *The Human Condition* (Chicago: University of Chicago Press, 1958), 236–43. Arendt ascribes to Jesus the discovery of the social role of forgiveness. But this was surely already developed in Judaism, as in the Book of Jonah, which Jesus himself cites in reference to the repentance of entire cities (Matt. 12:41).

2. "I will still speak out," interview with Leah Rabin, *Newsweek* (10 June 1996), 38.

3. L. P. Aguirre, "Breaking the Cycle of Evil," *Fellowship* 60 (July/Aug. 1994): 9.

4. K. Nürnberger and J. Tooke, *The Cost of Reconciliation in South Africa* (Cape Town: Methodist Publishing House, 1988), 112.

5. D. Krieger, "Law, Reconciliation, and Peacemaking," *Fellowship* 61 (July/Aug. 1995): 22.

6. Rabbi Leo Baeck, cited in *Fellowship* 60 (July/Aug. 1994): 10.

7. Luke 15:1-7, 8-10, 11-32; Matt. 5:43-48//Luke 6:27-28, 32-36; Matt. 5:21-24; Matt. 6:12//Luke 11:4; Mark 1:15 par.; Matt. 5:3-12//Luke 6:20-23; Mark 2:15-17 par.; Matt. 11:19//Luke 7:34; Matt. 11:28-30; Matt. 18:21-22//Luke 17:4; Matt. 18:23-35; Matt. 20:1-16; Luke 19:1-10. So also, the Beatitudes declare Jesus' hearers blessed prior to their fulfilling the rigorous demands of the gospel.

8. J. M. Lochman, *Reconciliation and Liberation* (Philadelphia: Fortress Press, 1980), 77.

9. D. Donnelly, *Learning to Forgive* (New York: Macmillan, 1979), 97–99.

10. K. Jaspers, "The Question of German Guilt" (1948), in *Transitional Justice: How Emerging Democracies Reckon with Former Regimes*, 3 vols., ed. Neil J. Kritz (Washington, D.C.: U.S. Institute of Peace, 1995), 1:159–60. This work of 2,323 pages is an invaluable resource.

11. R. J. Schreiter, *Reconciliation* (Maryknoll, N.Y.: Orbis Books, 1992), 71.

12. C. T. Boom, *The Hiding Place* (Old Tappan, N.J.: Revell Books, 1971), 238.

13. See Arendt, *The Human Condition*, 241. The reference is to Matt. 18:6.

14. S. Cassidy, quoted without reference by D. D. Risher, "The Way to God," *The Other Side* 31 (Nov./Dec. 1995): 11.

15. N. O'Brien, *Island of Tears, Island of Hope* (Maryknoll, N.Y.: Orbis Books, 1993), 139–40.

16. Cited by K. K. Chandy, *The Attitude to Property* (Manganam, Kottayam, India: Ashram Press, 1983), 26–27.

17. Cited by R. Kraybill, *Peaceskills: A Manual for Community Mediators* (Cape Town: Centre for Intergroup Studies, 1994), 75.

18. See W. Wink, *Violence and Nonviolence in South Africa* (Philadelphia: New Society Publishers, 1987), 5–10.

19. *The Christian Century* 112 (12 Apr. 1995): 387. In November 1995 the ABC National Ministries Board voted to reestablish ties with the BPF.

20. J. Cabazares, cited by N. O'Brien, *Island of Tears, Island of Hope*, 138.

21. E. Luttwak, "Franco-German Reconciliation: The Overlooked Role of the Moral Re-armament Movement," in *Religion, the Missing Dimension of Statecraft*, ed. D. Johnson and C. Sampson (New York: Oxford University Press, 1994), 37–57.

22. See Kraybill, *Peaceskills*, 75.

23. W. R. Callahan, "City of Hope and Reconciliation: Mothers of Matagalpa," *Fellowship* 60 (July/August 1994): 17.

24. "KKK" stands for the Ku Klux Klan, a racist hate group formed to terrorize blacks in the American South, but which has extended its hatred to Jews and certain foreign immigrants.

25. D. O'Reilly, "Converting the Klansman," *Philadelphia Enquirer* (9 Apr. 1995), H1, 6. This is a summary based on K. Wat-

terson, *Not by the Sword* (New York: Simon & Schuster, 1995), which tells the story in detail.

26. G. K. Hoffman, *No Royal Road to Reconciliation*, Patterns in Reconciliation, no. 2 (Alkmaar: IFOR, 1994), 33.

27. N. J. Kritz, "The Dilemmas of Transitional Justice," in *Transitional Justice*, 1: xxi–xxii.

Chapter Three: Issues of Reconciliation

1. J. Benomar, "Justice after Transitions," in *Transitional Justice: How Emerging Democracies Reckon with Former Regimes*, 3 vols., ed. Neil J. Kritz (Washington, D.C.: U.S. Institute of Peace, 1995), 1:34.

2. L. Weschler, *A Miracle, a Universe: Settling Accounts with Torturers* (New York: Pantheon Books, 1990), 4.

3. L. Weschler, "Afterword," *State Crimes: Punishment or Pardon* (Queenstown, Md.: Aspen Institute, 1988), 91–92.

4. S. Duncan, "National Unity and Reconciliation in the New South Africa," *Fellowship* 60 (July/Aug. 1994): 4.

5. R. J. Enquist, "Politics of Reconciliation, Namibian Style," *The Christian Century* 112 (15 Mar. 1995): 300.

6. Ibid., 301.

7. Kathleen Kern, "Haiti Two Years Later: Guns to Its Head," *The Nonviolent Activist* (Sept./Oct. 1996), 4–5.

8. R. Pagnucco and F. Teplitz, *Liberating Nonviolence: The Role of Servicio Paz Y Justicia in the Argentine and Uruguayan Transitions to Democracy* (Notre Dame, Ind.: The Joan B. Kroc Institute for International Peace Studies, n.d.), 24.

9. See Weschler, *A Miracle, a Universe*, 154–55, 235 on SERPAJ; on repeal of the impunity law, see pp. 175–236. See also "Uruguay," in *Transitional Justice*, 2:383–430.

10. See Weschler, *A Miracle, a Universe*, 171–72.

11. D. Coble and M. Pacenza, "Guatemala: Prospects for Peace," *Witness for Peace* (June 1995), 3–4.

12. R. Falla, S.J., *Massacres in the Jungle* (Boulder: Westview Press, 1994).

13. P. Jeffrey, "Telling the Truth," *The Christian Century* 112 (30 Aug.–6 Sept., 1995): 804–06; M. Popkin and N. Roht-Arriaza,

"Truth as Justice: Investigatory Commissions in Latin America," in *Transitional Justice*, 1:267–68.

14. D. Bronkhorst, *Truth and Reconciliation: Obstacles and Opportunities for Human Rights* (Amsterdam: Amnesty International Dutch Section, 1995), 75.

15. P. B. Hayner, "Fifteen Truth Commissions—1974–1994: A Comparative Study," in *Transitional Justice*, 241–42, 248, 254, 256; and Popkin and Roht-Arriaza in "Truth as Justice," in ibid., 1:262–89.

16. M. Specter, "If Poet's Room Could Speak, It Would Tell of Grief," *New York Times* (28 June 1995).

17. The West German government established by the Allies after World War II continued to prosecute former Nazis for various crimes. By 1970 some 12,900 persons had been prosecuted; 5,200 had been imprisoned, 76 of these for life. D. W. Shriver Jr., *An Ethic for Enemies* (New York: Oxford University Press, 1995), 82.

18. The civil government that succeeded the military in Greece set a six-month deadline on the filing of private prosecutions of high-level officials, and a three-month deadline for suits against other officials. These prosecutions provoked military discontent, but their response was far less destabilizing than what happened in Argentina. D. F. Orentlicher, "Settling Accounts: The Duty to Prosecute Human Rights Violations of a Prior Regime," in *Transitional Justice*, 2:405. Carlos S. Nino challenges Orentlicher's comparison of Argentina with Greece; the crimes in Argentina were so egregious that the public would have rejected so brief a window for prosecutions. "Response: The Duty to Punish Past Abuses of Human Rights Put into Context: The Case of Argentina," in ibid., 2:421.

19. J. Malamud-Goti, "Trying Violators of Human Rights: The Dilemma of Transitional Democratic Governments," in *State Crimes*, 76, 83.

20. See ibid., 57.

21. See ibid., 48–65; also Nino, "The Case of Argentina," in *Transitional Justice*, 2:323–81.

22. The U.N. Convention Against Torture precludes persons in signatory countries from enacting an amnesty law that forecloses

prosecution of torturers: See Orentlicher, "Settling Accounts," in *Transitional Justice*, 1:391.

23. S. P. Huntington, "The Third Wave: Democratization in the Late Twentieth Century," in *Transitional Justice*, 1:79.

24. *Time* (27 Mar. 1995), 47.

25. "Bishops Repent Role in "Dirty War,'" *The Christian Century* 112 (10 May 1995): 505–06; E. F. Mignone, *Witness to the Truth: The Complicity of Church and Dictatorship in Argentina 1976–1983* (Maryknoll, N.Y.: Orbis Books, 1988).

26. F. A. Rojas, "No Impunity in Chile," *Reconciliation International* 11 (June 1996): 3–4; see Bronkhorst, *Truth and Reconciliation*, 93.

27. See Popkin and Roht-Arriaza, "Truth as Justice," in *Transitional Justice*, 1:284–87.

28. J. Zalaquett, "Chile," in *Dealing with the Past*, eds. A. Boraine and J. L. & R. Scheffer (Cape Town: IDASA, 1994), 47–53; see Hayner, "Fifteen Truth Commissions," in *Transitional Justice*, 1:235–37; and "Chile," in ibid., 2:453–509.

29. See Hayner, "Fifteen Truth Commissions," in *Transitional Justice*, 1:226.

30. Weschler, *A Miracle, a Universe*, 246.

31. Peter Storey, "A Different Kind of Justice: Truth and Reconciliation in South Africa," *The Christian Century* 114 (Sept. 10–17, 1997): 790.

32. Ibid., 793.

33. Sheena Duncan, fax to author, 9 January 1996.

34. S. Holmes, "The End of Decommunization," in *Transitional Justice*, 1:116; *Berkshire Eagle* (26 Nov. 1995), A4.

35. See Bronkhorst, *Truth and Reconciliation*, 81–82.

36. L. Huyse, "Justice after Transitions: On the Choices Successor Elites Make in Dealing with the Past," in *Transitional Justice*, 1:104–15.

37. See Holmes, "The End of Decommunization," in *Transitional Justice*, 1:118.

38. See N. J. Kritz, ed., *Transitional Justice*.

39. J. Zalaquett, "Balancing Ethical Imperatives and Political Constraints: The Dilemma of New Democracies Confronting Past Human Rights Violations," in *Transitional Justice*, 2:495-96.

40. N. Tavuchis, *Mea Culpa: A Sociology of Apology and Reconciliation* (Stanford: Stanford University Press, 1991).

41. Ibid., 150.

42. Ibid., 110–17. A similar event took place when the Southern Baptist Convention (SBC) paused from its internecine conflicts long enough to apologize to all African Americans for slavery and for "condoning and/or perpetuating individual and systemic racism in our lifetime." The president of the second largest African American Baptist denomination rejected the apology as belated and needing to be backed up with actions against racism. Furthermore, said President Edward Jones, he was suspicious that the SBC was jockeying to win members of the fast-growing black middle class. *The Christian Century* 112 (27 Sept.–4 Oct. 1995): 879–80.

43. See Shriver, *An Ethic for Enemies*, 84–92.

44. *Newsweek* (8 May 1995), 51.

45. "Radiation Victims Get Clinton Apology," *Berkshire Eagle* (4 Oct. 1995), 3A.

46. *Peace Media Service* (Mar. 1995), 8.

47. *Berkshire Eagle* (8 Feb. 1996), A12.

48. G. K. Hoffman, "Forgiveness: Next Rung on the Peace Ladder?" *Fellowship* 60 (July/Aug. 1994): 14.

49. E. Lomax, *The Railway Man* (New York: W. W. Norton, 1995).

50. S. Lyall, "For Ex-British P.O.W., Forgiveness of a Japanese," *New York Times* (20 Aug. 1995), 10. Not all veterans were able to forgive. Three Australian former POWs held a counter-commemoration at the bridge and condemned their Japanese torturers. One said that if he saw a Japanese veteran, he would throw him off the bridge. *Berkshire Eagle* (21 Aug. 1995), A8.

51. "Japan's Prime Minister Apologizes to Asians," *Berkshire Eagle* (16 Aug. 1995), 2. For a thorough treatment, see Shriver, *An Ethic for Enemies*, 119–69.

52. See Shriver, *An Ethic for Enemies*, 141–42.

53. Ibid., 155–67.

54. How ironic, then, that at the same time as nations are learning to repent, corporations, doctors, manufacturers, and educators are being told by their lawyers never to admit to any wrong for fear of litigation.

Chapter Four: Toward Democracy

1. P. Storey, "South Africa's Election 'Miracle,'" *Life and Peace Review* (Jan. 1995), 9–11, as well as conversation with the author. Three radical black groups, the PAC, AZAPO, and WOSA, opposed the Accords and refused to sit at table with the others. Their reasons were powerfully cogent on almost every point, and yet in reality they were proven wrong. What had happened is that, contrary to all experience previously, most whites negotiated in good faith. See *The National Peace Accord: What Was Agreed To? And What Should Be Done about It?* Workers Organization for Socialist Action (*Worker's Voice*, Occasional Pamphlet No. 1, Oct. 1991).

2. ERJ was created by a coalition of church leaders and Christian trainers with the assistance of Bob and Alice Evans of Plowshares Institute. See the *Plowshares Newsletter* for Spring 1995 (P. O. Box 243, Simsbury, CT 06070). For a full report, see their "Evaluation and Final Report, Empowering for Reconciliation with Justice, Jan. 1991–Mar. 1995."

3. The term "critical solidarity" was apparently first coined under the communist regime in East Germany by Bishop Krusche of Magdeburg, and was given currency by his protege Heino Falcke. It had connotations in that context that are not appropriate to South Africa, since it involved accepting as fundamentally sound (and needing only criticism) a system that was intrinsically unjust, antireligious, and inhuman. See R. F. Goeckel, *The Lutheran Church and the East German State* (Ithaca, N.Y.: Cornell University Press, 1990), 174–75.

4. B. B. Bunker and B. T. Alban, "Editors' Introduction: The Large Group Intervention—A New Social Innovation?"; K. D. Dannemiller and R. W. Jacobs, "Changing the Way Organizations Change: A Revolution of Common Sense," both in Special Issue: *Large Group Interventions, Journal of Applied Behavioral Science* 28 (Dec. 1992): 473–98; see the whole issue. I have also benefited from an unpublished paper by Thomas A. Michael, "Creating New Cultures: The Contribution of Social Dreaming," delivered at the Symposium on International Perspectives on Organizations in Times of Turbulence, Swinburne University of Technology, Melbourne, Australia, 12 Aug. 1993.

5. This helpful distinction was introduced by R. Eisler, in *The Chalice and the Blade* (San Francisco: Harper & Row, 1987), 105. Eisler rightly sees hierarchy as neutral, and omnipresent in the biology of life. What matters is how hierarchy is used. In a domination hierarchy, the people serve the leader. In an enabling hierarchy, the leader serves the people.

6. See Dannemiller and Jacobs, "Changing the Way Organizations Change," 482.

7. M. Mpumlwana, "African Democracy and Grass Roots Conflict Resolution," ed. K. Nürnberger, *A Democratic Vision for South Africa*, NIR Reader, no. 3 (Pietermaritzburg: Encounter Publications, 1991), 376–84. The same pattern characterizes most Native American communities. In many cases, unfortunately, only males are regarded as stakeholders.

8. We need to recognize that greed is dysfunctional economically. Adam Smith condemned making profit the bottom line for a business. The bottom line, he said, is to serve the public welfare. Profit is the reward a company gets for serving the public welfare. Billie Alban shared this: a Japanese auto executive recognized the precise moment that his company would surpass General Motors. It was when the head of GM said, "We are not in the business of making cars. We're in the business of making money."

Bibliography

The following bibliography is only a fraction of the relevant titles. I have identified some books below as having a useful bibliography ("Bib."). See especially the work by Neil J. Kritz. Articles relevant to this study appear in almost all issues of Fellowship and Reconciliation International.

Ackerman, Peter, and Christopher Kruegler. *Strategic Nonviolent Conflict: The Dynamics of People Power in the Twentieth Century.* London: Praeger, 1994. Bib.

Alberts, L., and Frank Chikane. *The Road to Rustenburg: The Church Looking Forward to a New South Africa.* Cape Town: Struik Christian Books, 1991.

Aliaga Rojas, Fernando. "No Impunity in Chile." *Reconciliation International* no. 11 (June 1996): 3–4.

Alinsky, Saul. *Rules for Radicals.* New York: Random House, 1971.

Alperovitz, Gar. "Building a Living Democracy." *Sojourners* 19 (1990): 10–23.

Americas Watch. *Truth and Partial Justice in Argentina.* New York: The Americas Watch Committee, Aug. 1987.

Aguirre, Luis Pérez. "Breaking the Cycle of Evil." *Fellowship* 60 (July/Aug. 1994).

Arendt, Hannah. *The Human Condition.* Chicago: University of Chicago Press, 1958.

Barry, Tom. *Roots of Rebellion: Land and Hunger in Central America.* Boston: South End Press, 1987.

Baum, Gregory, and Harold Wells, eds. *The Reconciliation of Peoples.* Maryknoll, N.Y.: Orbis Books, 1997.

Berryman, Phillip. *Liberation Theology: The Essential Facts about the Revolutionary Movement in Latin America and Beyond.* New York: Pantheon Books, 1987.

Boesak, Alan. *Black and Reformed: Apartheid, Liberation, and the Calvinist Tradition.* Maryknoll, N.Y.: Orbis Books, 1984.

Boraine, Alex, Janet Levy, and Ronel Scheffer, eds. *Dealing with the Past: Truth and Reconciliation in South Africa.* Cape Town: IDASA, 1994.

Borer, Tristan. "Challenging the State: Churches as Political Actors in South Africa." *Journal of Church and Society* 35 (1993): 299–333.

Botha, Jan. *Versoening: in die Bybel en in die praktyk van die huiden Africa.* Potchefstroom, South Africa: Institut fir Reformatorie Studie, 1988.

Botman, H., and Robin M. Petersen. *To Remember and to Heal: Theological and Psychological Reflections on Truth and Reconciliation.* Cape Town: Human & Rousseau, 1996.

Bronkhorst, Daan. *Truth and Reconciliation: Obstacles and Opportunities for Human Rights.* Amsterdam: Amnesty International Dutch Section, 1995. Bib.

Buttry, Daniel. *Christian Peacemaking.* Valley Forge, Pa.: Judson Press, 1994.

Building Social Change Communities. The Training/Action Affinity Group. Philadelphia: New Society Publishers, 1979.

Bunker, Barbara Benedict, and Billie T. Alban, eds. *Large Group Interventions.* Special Issue. *Journal of Applied Behavioral Science* 28 (Dec. 1992).

Burgess, John P. "Church in East Germany Helps Create 'die Wende,'" *The Christian Century* 106 (6 Dec. 1989): 1140–42.

———. "Church-State Relations in East Germany: The Church as a

'Religious' and 'Political' Force." *Journal of Church and Society* 32 (1990): 17–35.

Cahill, Lisa Sowle. *Love Your Enemies: Discipleship, Pacifism, and Just War Theory.* Minneapolis: Fortress Press, 1994.

Callahan, William, R. "City of Hope and Reconciliation: Mothers of Matagalpa." *Fellowship* 60 (July/Aug. 1994): 17.

Carroll, J. J., S.J. "The Philippine Bishops: Pastors or Politicos?" *Human Society Booklet,* no. 37. Manila: Human Development Research and Documentation, 1987.

Casarjian, Robin. *Forgiveness.* New York: Bantam Books, 1992.

"Church and Stasi." *The Christian Century* 109 (Jan. 29, 1992): 89.

Coble, Dan, and Matt Pacenza. "Guatemala: Prospects for Peace." *Witness for Peace* (June 1995): 3–4.

Collins, Joseph. *The Philippines: Fire on the Rim.* San Francisco: Food First, 1989.

Comblin, José. *The Church and the National Security State.* Maryknoll, N.Y.: Orbis Books, 1984.

Conway, John S. "The Political Role of German Protestantism." *Journal of Church and State* 34 (1992): 819–41.

———. "The "Stasi" and the Churches: Between Coercion and Compromise in East German Protestantism, 1949-89." *Journal of Church and State* 36 (1992): 725–45.

Corradi, Juan E., Patricia Weiss Fagen, and Manuel Antonio Garreton, eds. *Fear at the Edge: State Terror and Resistance in Latin America.* Berkeley: University of California Press, 1992.

Cranston, Maurice. *What Are Human Rights?* New York: Basic Books, 1962.

Dahrendorf, Sir Ralf Gustav. "Roads to Freedom: Democratization and its Problems in East Central Europe." *Uncaptive Minds* 3/2 (Mar.–Apr. 1990): 1ff.

Dear, John. *The God of Peace: Toward a Theology of Nonviolence.* Maryknoll, N.Y.: Orbis Press, 1994.

La Defensa de los Derechos Humanos en la Transicion Democratica Uruguaya. Cuadernos Paz y Justicia, no. 4. Servicio Paz y Justicia-Uruguay, 1988.

Diamond, Larry, Juan J. Linz, and Seymour Martin Lipset, eds. *Democracy in Developing Countries.* 4 vols. Boulder: Lynne Rienner Publishers, 1990.

Donnelly, Doris. *Learning to Forgive.* New York: Macmillan, 1979.

Dorr, Donal. *Option for the Poor: A Hundred Years of Vatican Social Teaching.* Rev. ed. Maryknoll, N.Y.: Orbis Books, 1992.

Douglass, James W. *The Nonviolent Coming of God.* Maryknoll, N.Y.: Orbis Books, 1991.

Dugard, John. *Human Rights and the South African Legal Order.* Princeton, N.J.: Princeton University Press, 1978.

Duncan, Sheena. "National Unity and Reconciliation in the New South Africa." *Fellowship* 60 (July/Aug. 1994).

Du Toit, André. *Towards Democracy: Building a Culture of Accountability in South Africa.* Cape Town: IDASA, 1991.

Eisler, Riane. *The Chalice and the Blade.* San Francisco: Harper & Row, 1987.

Elwood, Douglas J., ed. *Toward a Theology of People Power: Reflections on the Philippine February Phenomenon.* Quezon City, Philippines: New Day Publishers, 1988.

Empowering for Reconciliation with Justice has produced training manuals for workshops on conflict resolution, mediation and negotiation for South Africa's emerging democracy. They are Anita Kromberg and Richard Steele, *Reconciliation: Building a More Peaceful and Democratic Society;* Crag Arendse et al., *Case Study Resource Packet;* Ron Kraybill, *Peaceskills: A Manual for Community Mediators;* and *Negotiation Trainer Manual,* Wilgespruit Fellowship Centre (Simsbury, Conn.: Plowshares Institute, 1995).

Enquist, Roy J. "Politics of Reconciliation, Namibian Style." *The Christian Century* 112 (Mar. 15, 1995): 300.

Falla, Ricardo, S.J. *Massacres in the Jungle.* Boulder: Westview Press, 1994.

Foster, Don. *Detention and Torture in South Africa: Psychological, Legal and Historical Studies.* New York: St. Martin's Press, 1987.

Gabanyi, Anneli Ute. *Die Unvollendete Revolution.* Munich: Piper, 1990.

Garcia, Ed. *Building Peace in the Philippines.* Tokyo: United National University, 1993.

———. *Participation in Governance: The People's Right.* Quezon City, Philippines: Claretian Publications, 1993.

Garton-Ash, Timothy. *The Polish Revolution: Solidarity.* New York: Scribners, 1983.

Gaspar, Karl M., C.S.S.R. *A People's Option: To Struggle for Creation.* Quezon City, Philippines: Claretian Publications, 1990.

Gillespi, Charles. "From Authoritarian Crises to Democratic Transitions." *Latin American Research Review* 22 (1987): 165–84.

Goeckel, Robert F. *The Lutheran Church and the East German State.* Ithaca, N.Y.: Cornell University Press, 1990. Bib.

Gomez, Fausto, O.P., et al. *The Philippine Revolution and the Involvement of the Church.* Manila: Social Research Center, University of Santo Tomas, 1986.

Gonzalez, Luis E. *Political Structures and Democracy in Uruguay.* Notre Dame: University of Notre Dame Press, 1991.

Gorringe, Timothy. *God's Just Vengeance: Crime, Violence, and the Rhetoric of Salvation.* Cambridge, England,: Cambridge University Press, 1996.

Goss-Mayr, Jean, and Hildegard Goss-Mayr. *The Gospel and the Struggle for Peace.* Alkmaar: International Fellowship of Reconciliation, 1990.

Green, Barbara G. "Looking Back on a Closing Chapter: The Experience of the East German Churches." *Theology and Public Policy* 3 (1991): 51–65.

Green, Paula. "Reconciliation: The Final Step." *Reconciliation International* 11 (June 1996): 1–3.

Havel, Václav. *Power of the Powerless.* London: Hutchison, 1985.

Hawkes, Nigel, ed. *Tearing Down the Curtain.* London: Hodder & Stoughton, 1990.

Hennelly, Alfred, and John Langan. *Human Rights in the Americas: The Struggle for Consensus.* Washington, D.C.: Georgetown University Press, 1982.

Higley, John, and Richard Gunther, eds. *Elites and Democratic Consolidation in Latin America and Southern Europe.* New York: Cambridge University Press, 1992.

Hill, Kent. *And the Wall Came Tumbling Down! The Role of Religion in the East German Revolution 1989–1990.* Washington, D.C.: Institute on Religion and Democracy, 1991.

Hoffman, Gene Knudsen. *No Royal Road to Reconciliation.* Patterns in Reconciliation, no. 2. Alkmaar: International Fellowship of Reconciliation, 1994.

———. "Forgiveness: Next Rung on the Peace Ladder?" *Fellowship* 60 (July/Aug. 1994).

Holland, Joe, and Peter Henriot, S.J. *Social Analysis: Linking Faith and Justice.* Maryknoll, N.Y.: Orbis Books, 1985.

Hope, Anne, and Sally Timmel. *Community Workers' Handbook: Training for Transformation.* The Grail, 2 Loch Avenue, Parktown 2193, South Africa, 1988.

Houver, Gerard. *A Non-Violent Lifestyle.* London: Marshall Morgan and Scott/Lamp Press, 1989.

Howard, Rhoda. "Evaluating Human Rights in Africa: Some Problems of Implicit Comparisons." *Human Rights Quarterly,* no. 6 (May 1984).

Hull, William E. *Beyond the Barriers.* Nashville: Broadman Press, 1981.

Hurley, Michael, S.J. *Reconciliation in Religion and Society: Proceedings of a Conference Organized by the Irish School of Ecumenics at the University of Ulster.* Belfast: Institute of Irish Studies, Queens University, 1994.

Jeffrey, Paul. "Telling the Truth." *The Christian Century* 112 (30 Aug.–6 Sep. 1995).

Jenco, Lawrence Martin, O.S.M. *Bound to Forgive: The Pilgrimage to Reconciliation of a Beirut Hostage.* Notre Dame, Ind.: Ave Maria Press, 1995.

Johnston, Douglas, and Cynthia Sampson. *Religion, The Missing Dimension of Statecraft.* New York: Oxford University Press, 1994.

Jones, L. Gregory. *Embodying Forgiveness: A Theological Analysis.* Grand Rapids: Wm. B. Eerdmans, 1995.

The Kairos Document: Challenge to the Church. Braamfontein: The Kairos Theologians, 1985.

Kelman, Herbert C., and D. P. Warwick, eds. *The Ethics of Social Intervention.* Washington, D.C.: Halstead Press, 1978.

Kraybill, Ron. *Peaceskills: A Manual for Community Mediators.* Cape Town: Centre for Intergroup Studies (37 Grotto Rd., Rondebosch 7700 Cape Town, South Africa), 1994.

Krieger, David. "Law, Reconciliation, and Peacemaking." *Fellowship* 61 (July/Aug. 1995).

Kritz, Neil J. *Transitional Justice: How Emerging Democracies Reckon with Former Regimes.* 3 vols. Washington, D.C.: United States Institute of Peace, 1995.

Küng, Hans. *Global Responsibility: In Search of a New World Ethic.* New York: Crossroad, 1991.

Lakey, George. *Powerful Peacemaking: A Strategy for a Living Revolution.* Philadelphia: New Society Publishers, 1987.

Lategan, Bernard, et al. *The Option for Inclusive Democracy: A Theological-Ethical Study of Appropriate Social Values for South Africa.* Stellenbosch: Centre for Hermeneutics, Stellenbosch University, 1987.

Lehmann, Paul. *The Transfiguration of Politics.* New York: Harper & Row, 1975.

Lerner, Michael. *Surplus Powerlessness.* London: Humanities Press International, 1986.

Linden, Ian. *The Catholic Church and the Struggle for Zimbabwe.* London: Longman, 1980.

Lissner, Jorgen, and Aren Sovik, eds. *A Lutheran Reader on Human Rights.* Geneva: Lutheran World Federation, 1978.

Lomax, Eric. *The Railway Man.* New York: W. W. Norton, 1995.

Lopez, George, and Michael Stohl, eds. *Liberalization and Redemocratization in Latin America.* New York: Greenwood Press, 1987.

Lovett, Brendan. *On Earth as in Heaven: Corresponding to God in the Philippine Context.* Quezon City, Philippines: Claretian Publications, 1988.

Malamud-Goti, Jaime. "Trying Violators of Human Rights: The Dilemma of Transitional Democratic Governments." *State Crimes: Punishment or Pardon.* Queenstown, Md.: The Justice and Society Program of Aspen Institute, 1988.

Mastellone, Flavia Rose. *Finding Peace through Conflict: Teaching Skills for Resolving Conflicts and Building Peace.* Amherst, Mass.: National Association for Mediation in Education, 1993. Bib.

McGovern, Arthur F. *Liberation Theology and Its Critics: Toward an Assessment.* Maryknoll, N.Y.: Orbis Books, 1989.

McManus, Philip, and Gerald Schlabach. *Relentless Persistence: Non-*

violent Action in Latin America. Philadelphia: New Society Publishers, 1991.

McSorley, Richard. *The New Testament Basis of Peacemaking*. Scottdale, Pa.: Herald Press, 1979.

Meacham, Carl E. "The Role of the Chilean Catholic Church in the New Chilean Democracy." *Journal of Church and State* 36 (Spring 1994): 277–99.

Merton, Thomas. *Faith and Violence*. South Bend, Ind.: Notre Dame University Press, 1965.

Michnik, Adam. *Letters from Prison and Other Essays*. Berkeley: University of California Press, 1986.

Mignone, Emilio F. *Witness to the Truth: The Complicity of Church and Dictatorship in Argentina 1976–1983*. Maryknoll, N.Y.: Orbis Books, 1988.

Miller, Allen O., ed. *A Christian Declaration on Human Rights*. Grand Rapids: Wm. B. Eerdmans, 1977.

Miller-Fahrenholz, Geiko. *The Art of Forgiveness*. Geneva: WCC Publications, 1997.

Moll, Peter, Nico Nattrass, and Lieb Loots, eds. *Redistribution: How Can It Work in South Africa?* Cape Town: David Philips, 1991.

Mott, Stephen C. *Biblical Ethics and Social Change*. New York: Oxford University Press, 1982.

Mpumlwana, Malusi. "African Democracy and Grass Roots Conflict Resolution." *A Democratic Vision for South Africa*. Klaus Nürnberger, ed. NIR Reader no. 3. Pietermaritzburg, South Africa: Encounter Publications, 1991.

Muhaiyaddeen, M. R. Bawa. *Islam and World Peace: Explanations of a Sufi*. Philadelphia: Fellowship Press, 1987.

Muller, Alois, and Norbert Greinacher. *The Church and the Rights of Man*. New York: Seabury Press, 1979.

Murphy, Jeffrie G., and Jean Hampton. *Forgiveness and Mercy*. Cambridge: Cambridge University Press, 1988.

Musto, Ronald G. *The Catholic Peace Tradition*. Maryknoll, N.Y.: Orbis Books, 1986. Bib.

Nielsen, Niels C. *Revolutions in Eastern Europe: The Religious Roots*. Maryknoll, N.Y.: Orbis Books, 1991.

Nowak, Kurt. "Der Protestantismus in der DDR-Erfahrungen und

Schwierigkeiten auf dem Weg zur Democratie"["Protestantism in the Experience of the DDR and Difficulties on the Road to Democracy"]. *Zeitschrift für Evangelische Ethik* 34 (1990): 165–73.

Nürnberger, Klaus. *A Democratic Vision for South Africa: Political Realism and Christian Responsibility.* Pietermaritzburg, South Africa: Encounter Publications, 1991.

———, and John Tooke. *The Cost of Reconciliation in South Africa.* Cape Town: Methodist Publishing House, 1988.

O'Brien, Niall. *Island of Tears, Island of Hope.* Maryknoll, N.Y.: Orbis Books, 1993. Bib.

———. *Revolution from the Heart.* New York: Oxford University Press, 1987.

O'Donnell, Guillermo, and Philippe C. Schmitter. *Transitions from Authoritarian Rule.* Vol. 4: *Tentative Conclusions about Uncertain Democracies.* Baltimore: Johns Hopkins University Press, 1986.

O'Gorman, Angie, ed. *The Universe Bends toward Justice: A Reader on Christian Nonviolence in the U.S.* Philadelphia: New Society Publishers, 1990.

O'Reilly, David. "Converting the Klansman." *Philadelphia Inquirer,* 9 Apr. 1995, H1, 6.

Pagnucco, Ron, and Fran Teplitz. *Liberating Nonviolence: The Role of Servicio Paz Y Justicia in the Argentine and Uruguayan Transitions to Democracy.* Notre Dame: Joan B. Kroc Institute, n.d.

Parkman, Patricia. *Insurrectionary Civic Strikes in Latin America 1931–1961.* Monograph Series no. 1. Cambridge, Mass.: Albert Einstein Institution, 1990.

Pattridge, Blake D. "The Catholic Church in Revolutionary Guatemala, 1944–54: A House Divided." *Journal of Church and State* 36 (1994): 527–40.

Penance and Reconciliation: International Bibliography. Strasbourg: Cedric Publications, 1984.

Pérez Aguirre, Luis. "Breaking the Cycle of Evil." *Fellowship* 60 (1994): 9.

Phillips, Derek. *Toward a Just Social Order.* Princeton, N.J.: Princeton University Press, 1986.

Pollack, Erwin H., ed. *Human Rights.* Buffalo: Jay Steward, 1971.

Pollis, Adamantia, and Peter Schwab, eds. *Human Rights: Cultural and Ideological Perspectives*. New York: Praeger, 1979.

Polner, Murray, and Naomi Goodman, eds. *The Challenge of Shalom: The Jewish Tradition of Peace and Justice*. Philadelphia: New Society Publishers, 1994.

Preston, Ronald H. *Church and Society in the Late Twentieth Century: The Economic and Political Task*. London: SCM Press, 1983.

Reconciliation: Reflections on the Occasion of IFOR's 75th Anniversary. Patterns in Reconciliation, no. 1. Alkmaar: International Fellowship of Reconciliation, 1994.

The Road to Damascus: Kairos and Conversion. A document signed by Third World Christians from El Salvador, Guatemala, Korea, Namibia, Nicaragua, Philippines, South Africa. London: Catholic Institute for International Relations, 1989.

Robertson, Mike. *Human Rights for South Africans*. Cape Town: Oxford University Press, 1991.

Rojas, Fernando Aliaga. "No Impunity in Chile." *Reconciliation International* 11 (June 1996).

Salmi, Jamil. *Violence & Democratic Society: New Approaches to Human Rights*. London: ZED Books, 1993.

Sawatsky, Walter. "Truth Telling in Eastern Europe." *Journal of Church and Society* 33 (1991): 701–29.

Schreiter, Robert J. *Reconciliation: Mission and Ministry in a Changing Social Order*. Maryknoll, N.Y.: Orbis Press, 1992.

Servicio Paz Y Justicia-Uruguay. *Uruguay: Nunca Más*. Philadelphia: Temple University Press, 1992.

Sharp, Gene. *The Politics of Nonviolent Action*. 3 vols. Boston: Porter Sargent, 1973.

Shaull, Richard. *Heralds of a New Reformation: The Poor of South and North America*. Maryknoll, N.Y.: Orbis Books, 1984.

Shenk, Gerald. *God With Us? The Roles of Religion in the Former Yugoslavia*. Uppsala: Life & Peace Institute, 1993.

Shriver, Donald. *An Ethic for Enemies*. New York: Oxford University Press, 1995. Bib.

Smith, Page. *Rediscovering Christianity: A History of Modern Democracy and the Christian Ethic*. New York: St. Martin's Press, 1994.

Solberg, R. W. *God and Caesar in East Germany: The Conflicts of*

Church and State in East Germany since 1945. New York: Macmillan, 1961.

The South African Handbook of Education for Peace. Cape Town: Quaker Peace Centre (3 Rye Road, Mowbray, Cape Town 7700, South Africa), 1992.

Stark, David, and Laszlo Bruszt. "Negotiating the Institutions of Democracy: Contingent Choices and Strategic Interactions in the Hungarian and Polish Transitions." *Cornell Working Papers on Transitions from State Socialism,* no. 8. Ithaca, N.Y.: Mario Einaudi Center for International Studies, Cornell University, 1990.

Stassen, Glen H. *Just Peacemaking.* Louisville: Westminster/John Knox, 1992.

State Crimes: Punishment or Pardon. The Justice and Society Program of Aspen Institute. Queenstown, Md.: Aspen Institute, 1988.

Storey, Peter. "A Different Kind of Justice: Truth and Reconciliation in South Africa." *The Christian Century* 114 (Sept. 10–17, 1997): 788–93.

———. "South Africa's Election 'Miracle.'" *Life and Peace Review* (Jan. 1995).

Swomley, John W., Jr. *Liberation Ethics.* New York: Macmillan, 1972.

Tavuchis, Nicholas. *Mea Culpa: A Sociology of Apology and Reconciliation.* Stanford: Stanford University Press, 1991.

Tischner, José F. *The Spirit of Solidarity.* San Francisco: Harper & Row, 1984.

Thistlethwaite, Susan, ed. *A Just Peace Church.* New York: United Church Press, 1986.

Track Two: Constructive Approaches to Community and Political Conflict. A quarterly publication of the Centre for Intergroup Studies, 37 Grotto Road, Rondebosch, Cape Town 7700, South Africa.

Umbreit, Mark. *Crime and Reconciliation: Creative Options for Victims and Offenders.* Nashville: Abingdon, 1985.

Vanderhaar, Gerard, and Janice Vanderhaar. *The Philippines: Agony and Hope.* Erie, Pa.: Pax Christi USA, 1989.

Villa-Vicencio, Charles. "The Road to Reconciliation." *Sojourners* 26 (May–June, 1997): 34–38.

———. *A Theology of Reconstruction: Nation-Building and Human Rights.* Cambridge: Cambridge University Press, 1992. Bib.

Volf, Miroslav. *Exclusion and Embrace.* Nashville: Abingdon Press, 1996.

Watterson, Kathryn. *Not by the Sword.* New York: Simon & Schuster, 1995.

Weschler, Lawrence. *A Miracle, a Universe: Settling Accounts with Torturers.* New York: Pantheon Books, 1990.

———. "Afterword." *State Crimes: Punishment or Pardon.* Queenstown, Md.: Aspen Institute, 1988.

World Council of Churches. *Human Rights: A Challenge to Theology.* Rome: CIIA/WCC and IDOC International, 1983.

Wink, Walter. *Engaging the Powers: Discernment and Resistance in a World of Domination.* Minneapolis: Fortress Press, 1992.

———. "The Kingdom: God's Domination-free Order." *Weavings* 10 (1995): 6–15.

———. *Violence and Nonviolence in South Africa.* Philadelphia: New Society Publishers, 1987.

Yoder, Perry B., and Willard M. Swartley, eds. *The Meaning of Peace: Biblical Studies.* Louisville: Westminster/John Knox Press, 1992. Bib.

Youngblood, Robert L. *Marcos Against the Church.* Ithaca, N.Y.: Cornell University Press, 1990.

Zalaquett, José. "Chile," in *Dealing with the Past.* Alex Boraine, Janet Levy, and Ronel Scheffer, eds. Cape Town: IDASA, 1994.